P9-DFP-183

THE BASICS OF
BONDS

Gerald Krefetz

Dearborn
Financial Publishing, Inc.

While a great deal of care has been taken to provide accurate and current information, the ideas, suggestions, general principles and conclusions presented in this text are subject to local, state and federal laws and regulations, court cases and any revisions of same. The reader is thus urged to consult legal counsel regarding any points of law—this publication should not be used as a substitute for competent legal advice.

Publisher: Kathleen A. Welton
Associate Editor: Karen A. Christensen
Senior Project Editor: Jack L. Kiburz
Interior Design: Lucy Jenkins
Cover Design: Sam Concialdi

©1992 by Gerald Krefetz

Published by Dearborn Financial Publishing, Inc.

All rights reserved. The text of this publication, or any part thereof, may not be reproduced in any manner whatsoever without written permission from the publisher.

Printed in the United States of America

93 94 10 9 8 7 6 5 4 3 2

Library of Congress Cataloging-in-Publication Data

Krefetz, Gerald
    The basics of bonds / Gerald Krefetz.
        p. cm. — (Making the most of your money series)
    Includes index.
    ISBN 0-79310-360-6 (paper)
        1. Government securities—United States. 2. Bonds—United States.
    3. Investments—United States. I. Title. II. Series: Krefetz,
    Gerald. Making the most of your money series.
HG4941.K74 1992   91-42813
332.632'3—dc20   CIP

Dedication

To Dorothy, Nadine and Adriene

Contents

Introduction   ix

    Why Read This Book?   ix
    What You Should Save   x
    Figure Your Interest Rates   xii
    Know What Risk Means   xiv
    The Fixed-Income Investor   xvii
    The Lurking Danger   xviii
    A Word on the Organization of This Book   xix

**Chapter 1 • The World of Fixed-Income
Investments**   1

    What Are Bonds?   1
    Why Invest in Bonds Now?   4
    How Do Bonds Behave?   7
    Your Move   15

Chapter 2 • Figuring Bond Yields   17

    Which Yield Is Right for You?   17
    What Is the Total Return?   24
    All Yields Are Not Created Equal   26
    The Yield Curve and Interest Rates   28
    Your Move   34

Chapter 3 • Risk-Free Fixed-Income Investments Without Fluctuations   37

What You See Is What You Get   37
Money Market Accounts   38
Money Market Funds   40
Certificates of Deposit   43
U.S. Savings Bonds   45
Your Move   47

Chapter 4 • U.S. Governments: Risk-Free Investments with Fluctuations   49

U.S. Treasury Bills   49
U.S. Treasury Notes and Bonds   55
Zero Coupon Bonds   60
Your Move   66
Shortcut   66

Chapter 5 • Federal Agency Securities: Higher Government Interest Rates   69

Are They Different from Treasuries?   69
Mortgage-Backed Securities   76
Your Move   80
Shortcut   81

Chapter 6 • Municipal Bonds: Tax-Free Investing   83

The World of Munis   83
What Does Tax Exemption Mean to You?   87
All Munis Are Not Equal!   90
Buying Municipals   94
What about Interest?   96
Swapping: Gains and Losses   98
Your Move   99
Shortcut   101

Chapter 7 • Corporate Bonds **103**

High Yield, Some Risk 103
The Corporate World 107
Buying and Selling Bonds 109
Pricing 112
Ratings: A Matter of Quality 113
Enter Event Risk 117
At a Discount 119
Your Move 120
Shortcut 121

Chapter 8 • Convertible Bonds **123**

The Best of Both Worlds 123
The Case for Convertibles 126
A Call on the Common 128
Your Move 130
Shortcut 130

Chapter 9 • High-Yielding Corporate Bonds **131**

All about Junk Bonds 131
The Brave New World of Junk Bonds 133
Your Move 137
Shortcut 138

Chapter 10 • Planning Your Portfolio **139**

Do's 144
Don'ts 145

Appendix A • Yield to Maturity **147**

Appendix B • Characteristics of Selected Fixed-Income Investments **151**

Glossary **155**

Index **163**

Introduction

WHY READ THIS BOOK?

The purpose of this book is to assist you in making decisions with that portion of your personal wealth devoted to fixed-income investing. Everyone should save some of their disposable income throughout their working careers. Some individuals will also be lucky enough to inherit money or come into a windfall.

How you allocate those funds is a personal choice, conditioned by many variables. This book will help sort out those variables so that you can make intelligent decisions in a timely manner. Since this book is part of the series *Making the Most of Your Money,* it will occasionally refer to the other volumes for fuller explanations of ideas and concepts.

Fixed-income investing is an old and trustworthy idea. It is based on the simple idea that some of your saved money can be lent to others, whether they be individuals, institutions or government bodies.

In return, you obtain a promise (an IOU) that you will be paid interest on a regular basis, and that your money will be repaid at a certain time. All fixed-income investments are originally issued with this promise spelled out in legal terms. (Most of the investments discussed in this book are bonds. Strictly speaking, some are not, but they all have enough general characteristics so that the terms *fixed-income investments* and *bonds* are used almost interchangeably.)

The act of lending money is, of course, more complicated than this simple description suggests. You must deal with problems of interest rates, at what time interest is to be paid, the length of time the funds are to be lent, to whom the money is to be lent and for what purpose, the credibility of the borrowers, the tax consequences of the earned interest, etc.

Before you can answer these questions, you should review your personal financial situation as outlined in *The Basics of Investing*.

WHAT YOU SHOULD SAVE

Diligence requires you to analyze your current wealth, the funds or assets you now possess, and your future wealth, the funds or assets you hope to earn or inherit in the foreseeable future. To appreciate what you own and what you owe, you should draw up a net worth statement. A net worth statement presents a visual record of your progress in accumulating personal assets. The object of money management is to increase your wealth at a steady rate, perhaps 10 percent a year. The net worth statement should also tell you the present distribution of your assets, and whether you have sufficient funds to start an investment program.

Once you determine your net worth, you must also consider your age and your career status. The older you get, the more money you are likely to save. If your net worth indicates a number of assorted savings accounts squirreled here and there, it is time to order them in a fashion that will provide additional security. (Every year, thousands of bank accounts are turned over to state authorities when they are deemed to be inactive. Therefore, you should consolidate all savings accounts and make sure that at the very least interest is posted once a year.)

Once your passbook account exceeds $1,000, you should place all future savings in a money market account or a money market fund to obtain higher interest rates on your demand accounts.

For emergency purposes, you should always have three to six months, income in cash or its equivalent, such as a passbook or statement savings account.

Once your savings exceed one year's after-tax earnings or $20,000, whichever is greater, four-fifths of your funds should be in long-term deposits, such as certificates of deposit. The other one-fifth should be kept in demand accounts, which pay the highest rates of interest.

If you are 25 years of age and have a negative net worth or one of modest four figures, you should be saving 5–10 percent of your disposable income—perhaps more if you have no family. Your goal should be to save 10 percent of your gross income.

When your voluntary savings (not including savings accumulated in life insurance, home mortgage or pension) reach one year's salary, you should consider how to diversify for safety and the best return on your money.

If you are 45 years of age, it is not unlikely that your net worth now exceeds $100,000. While you may have $10,000 in common stock (either inherited or purchased from the corporation you work for), your savings are about $20,000. It is time to diversify, if you have not done so already. You should consider fixed-income investments and increasing your holdings of common stock to spread the risk and increase the rate of growth.

If you are 65 years of age, it is time to consider selling some common stock investments. With the proceeds, purchase more fixed-income investments to increase your retirement earnings.

FIGURE YOUR INTEREST RATES

Whether you ever buy a certificate of deposit or another fixed-income investment, you should know what rate of interest your money is earning. One of the keys to successful money management is to let interest rates work for you.

Interest on money can double and triple your funds in a relatively short time. Over a long period of time, the effect can be almost miraculous. Not long ago, *The Wall Street Journal* calculated that the $24 the Dutch paid the native Americans for Manhattan at compound interest at ordinary rates would equal the present assessed valuation of the real estate on that island.

Therefore, it is important to get the best interest rates over the longest possible time. (For a complete review of interest rate calculations see *The Basics of Investing*, Chapter 3.) For example, if you could save $2,000 a year at 10 percent tax-free, you would have $12,210 at the end of five years, and $114,550 at the end of 20 years.

As a rule, compound interest is better than simple interest, providing there is no difference in rates. The more frequent the compounding, the faster the principal and interest will grow.

After your savings have reached the equivalent of one year of your after-tax earnings, you should consider an investment program. A prudent and conservative investment program should consist primarily of common stocks and debt obligations, the former for growth and the latter for income. (If your assets are great enough, say in excess of $100,000, you might also consider real estate, collectibles, and precious metals for additional balance and safety.)

But before you undertake an investment program, you must analyze both your motives and your risk tolerance. It is true that "money makes money," but it is also true that money can be lost if the purpose of the investment is unclear or ill-conceived. Funds can also be lost if you take on undue risk, or to put it another way, if you assume more risk than you can stand.

In brief, it is possible to lose money if your attitude is unrealistic and your game plan is not suited to your temperament. For example, to expect the value of a common stock purchase to double in the course of a year is unreasonable. An equally unreasonable expectation is to reach for excessive interest rates with funds designated for fixed-income investments without exposing your money to chancy circumstances.

To be successful, you must be both realistic in terms of what has gone before (the normal precedents) and in appreciating your comfort zones (the level of risk you can tolerate).

To understand what kind of return you can expect on fixed-income investments, turn to either the business section of your daily newspaper, or to one of the financial dailies: *The Wall Street Journal* or *Investor's Business Daily*. In tabular form, you will find a listing of money rates for all classes of fixed-income investments. The list covers every kind of debt instrument, from ones that mature tomorrow to ones that are not due for 30 years.

Therefore, any fixed-income investment you consider making should have a comparative rate in the table. The same is true for savings instruments. The daily financial press or weekly magazines carry tables of what money market mutual funds are paying and what rates are being offered by banks for their certificates of deposit.

If you find a savings or debt instrument that is notably different from the average rates, you must ask yourself the reason for the disparity. It is a rule of thumb in finance that when interest rates differ from general averages, some important underlying cause can explain the abnormality.

In short, rates that are markedly different from average rates should be a cause for caution. If a savings and loan association is offering certificates of deposit at a half percent or a full percent above the competitive average, it may well be in difficult circumstances. It is offering higher rates to attract funds, perhaps because it is in financial trouble.

KNOW WHAT RISK MEANS

Rewards in the financial world are usually matched with risks. Therefore, it is imperative for you to determine how much risk you can tolerate.

In general, there are three kinds of risk personalities: The *risk lover* welcomes chancy situations. The *risk-averse* investor attempts to avoid any position whose outcome cannot be foretold. The *risk-neutral* individual is willing to live with some chancy outcome. For this person, risk neither creates anxiety nor causes pleasure.

It is important for you to analyze your own risk temperament in order to match your portfolio with your personality. A mismatch will cause irritation, anxiety and finally a loss of money.

Most of the time risk is taken to mean that the outcome of the investment situation is uncertain. In other words, risk is the deviation from an expected return on your money.

If you are a risk-averse investor, you will feel decidedly uncomfortable in an investment whose ultimate price cannot be defined before the investment is made. If you are a risk-neutral investor, you may expect the outcome of an investment decision to fall between a certain level of loss and gain. In either case, you will not be unduly concerned. If you are a risk lover, the very idea of an uncertain outcome is welcomed, giving as much pleasure as the actual result.

Risk in the financial world is caused by a number of different conditions. Three sources of risk are of particular concern to you, since they cause volatility, which is the chief characteristic of risk.

Interest rate risk arises from the constant change in the demand and supply of money. *Company risk* comes from a corporation's business activity. *Market risk* stems from conditions that impact the whole economy.

These three types of risk will affect your stock and bond holdings. You can take steps, however, to counterbalance their impact. (For some useful tactics in hedging these risks in common stock see *The Basics of Stocks,* Chapter 6.)

Some of the work measuring risk has been done for you by statistical rating agencies such as Standard & Poor's, Moody's, Value Line and others. These companies assign specific ratings to a wide range of common and preferred stock, and to fixed-income investments. A prudent investor will pay close attention to these independent, critical ratings.

Additional information comes from financial publications, newsletters and recommendations by investment banking firms. Computerized data bases such as CompuServe, the Dow Jones News Retrieval, Prodigy and Genie provide up-to-the-minute financial analyses and market quotations.

Your Money and Your Risk

If you do not have $20,000 or one year's earnings (whichever is greater) in secure savings instruments, you probably should not be in the securities markets. Your first obligation to yourself and your family is to have a nest egg, an inviolable fund of cash, come hell or high water.

Next, you must decide whether you intend to be an active or passive investor. If you intend to be a passive investor, you must choose who will act on your behalf. A passive investor has three possible choices to administer a portfolio: select a mutual fund, select an investment advisory service, or select a professional money manager.

The kind of mutual fund or professional counsel you choose should reflect your comfort level. Even a passive investor must make basic decision concerning risk tolerances.

The active investor is continually faced with risk decisions. However, both the active and passive investor must make some fundamental decisions as to what position or percentage of their portfolio holdings will be risk-free, what portion will harbor some risk and what portion will contain significant risk. (For a table of potential portfolios for different risk levels see *The Basics of Investing,* Chapter 7.)

If you intend to be a fixed-income investor, or expect to have a significant portion of your portfolio in these instruments, this book will explain the benefits and caution you about the pitfalls, of this type of investment.

You should invest only that portion of your savings that exceeds the $20,000 nest egg. While fixed-income investments are in general more conservative and stable than most stock holdings, they nevertheless do fluctuate in price. In an emergency, you may not be able to liquidate some of them without taking a loss.

Therefore, always safeguard your savings in some demand accounts that do not fluctuate in value and are not subject to any of the risks mentioned before. Do not confuse (or commingle) your savings accounts with fixed-income investments.

THE FIXED-INCOME INVESTOR

Investors wishing to invest in fixed-income securities are motivated by concerns of safety and income. If safety is your consideration, you will find a universe of debt obligations that are guaranteed by the U.S. government or various municipal authorities.

If you lend them your money—that is, purchase their IOUs—you (or your estate) will almost certainly have those funds returned when the obligations mature. Moreover, a broad secondary market exists for these securities so that they can be sold in a moment's notice to regain your funds before maturity.

If income is your chief concern, the investment-grade issues of the fixed-income universe will give you a steady and constant return on your funds. Since some issues pay interest monthly, while others pay quarterly or semiannually, you must search out which obligations are most suitable to your investment strategy.

The rates of interest on fixed-income investments naturally vary considerably and change on a daily basis. Long-term investors (a category that includes most investors in debt obligations) wish to lock in what they consider advantageous rates. In brief, they buy them and forget them.

Short-term investors in the bond market are less concerned about the interest that these obligations pay them than in the fluctuations of the principal. Bond prices usually do not vary as much as common stock prices. However, when interest rates rise, bond prices fall, and vice versa.

This inverse relationship is a powerful lever for moving the prices of fixed-income investments. If you are agile and attentive, you can take advantage of the fluctuations in the market and profit by trading bonds.

THE LURKING DANGER

If you intend to be a fixed-income investor, you should also be aware of the disadvantages of such investments. This is especially true if you expect to buy *only* such obligations. Careful portfolio planning calls for a mix of assets. If you rely on one type of investment to the exclusion of others, you forego the safety that a balanced portfolio provides.

Moreover, there is one overriding danger lurking in the fixed-income world. In a nutshell, you will receive back only interest and the return of your principal when the bonds come due or are sold.

In a world of crashing stock prices, fluctuating currency values, a shaky financial system, enormous corporate debts, and huge governmental deficits, you may be thankful just to receive back your funds. On the other hand, in an age of inflation, getting back your original principal is less than satisfactory if its purchasing power has seriously shrunk.

Therefore, proper portfolio balance calls for both common stock to provide asset growth, and bonds to provide income and additional safety. The balance, of course, is a personal consideration depending on age, family status, life-style, monetary responsibilities, career and other variables. Each investor must decide on the appropriate allocation of assets, that equilibrium of comfort.

Asset allocation naturally changes as you move through the stages of life. It should also change as the economy moves through the various stages of the business cycle. (For an overview of investing and the business cycle see *The Basics of Investing*, Chapter 15.)

The bond market is a valuable complement to the stock market. The following chapters will show you which of the fixed-income investments fit your needs. They will also indicate the advantages and disadvantages of each type of bond.

The bond market does not operate in a vacuum. Consequently, this book will reveal the important interaction among credit, interest rates, the money supply, the business cycle and the Federal Reserve System. If you understand this interaction, you will be better prepared to benefit at critical turning points in the market.

Finally, this book will show you how to trade bonds profitably and how to obtain the best return on your funds. It will also examine the benefits of tax-free instruments and how they can put more disposable income in your hands.

Without any loss of safety, the fixed-income market can increase your return on your money by 100 percent over conventional savings programs. Therefore, fixed-income investments deserve a place in your portfolio.

A WORD ON THE ORGANIZATION OF
THIS BOOK

This book is organized by the major fixed-income investment groups. The underlying assumption is simple: Fixed-income investors are primarily concerned with risk and price volatility of their investments. Therefore, the chapters are organized sequentially—from the risk-free, nonfluctuating accounts of the fixed-income investment world, to the volatile and unpredictable world of "junk" bonds. You must decide which type of account or debt obligation best meets your investment needs. Each subsequent chapter indicates slightly more risk or price fluctuations, or both.

A second assumption implicit in the book's organization is that there are *active* and *passive* investors. For the active investor, one who wishes to fully understand the mechanics and workings of the bond market, the whole chapter will provide information and guidance.

If you are a passive investor, one who wishes to either buy securities and put them away or simply wants an adequate understanding of these instruments, the introductory material provides a quick review of the important facts.

The material in this book is divided into five categories, based on the standard characteristics by which all fixed-income investments can be defined, identified and compared. For simplicity, each investment will be analyzed by description; risk and rating; maturity and duration; income and yield; and special benefits.

The *description* defines what kind of debt instrument you are purchasing, what are the general terms of the obligation, who issues or guarantees repayment of interest and principal and its relative position in the investment world.

Risk and rating draws attention to the elements of safety or danger inherent in such obligations. It indicates what you should look for, and what the rating services think about such issues.

Maturity and duration alerts you to the limit or span of the debt instrument's life. Some obligations have set maturities, while others have early call provisions, and still others may run forever.

Income and yield informs you what kind of return on the principal you may expect. It is important to be aware of three kinds of yields as well as yields of other comparable debt obligations.

Special benefits lets you know whether the obligation is tax-free or has some other tax advantage. It also indicates whether there are any other advantages that are out of the ordinary.

Shortcut

Following some sections, you will see the heading, "Shortcut." In these sections, you will find a number of bond funds that have tried-and-true performance records. These suggestions should not be considered an endorsement—only some of the more popular bond funds to be found in the marketplace.

• 1 •

The World of Fixed-Income Investments

WHAT ARE BONDS?

Fixed-income investments, or bonds, are long-term obligations issued by corporations, governments, agencies, regional authorities and municipalities. The issuer promises to pay the buyer of its bonds interest twice a year. The issuer also agrees to repay the loan at a fixed date in the future, usually in 15 or 20 years.

These promises are legally binding, and the bond's *trustee,* an independent bank or trust company acting on behalf of the investor, has these terms spelled out in the bond's *indenture.* Should the bond issuer not pay interest or return the principal on time, the trustee pursues whatever legal remedy may be appropriate.

Bonds and preferred stock are considered *senior securities*—they receive consideration for payment of interest before common stockholders received dividends. If the issuer runs into trouble, you, the bondholder, will be first in line for distribution of the company's assets. Creditors (bondholders) are paid before owners (stockholders).

Corporate bonds are generally issued in denominations of $1,000 (*par value*), but some municipal bonds are issued in denominations of $5,000, and some federal government debt is issued in $10,000 and $25,000 units.

Each bond has a *coupon rate,* a fixed rate of interest it will pay throughout the life of the security. How you will be paid your interest depends on whether the issue is a registered or bearer bond.

If it is a registered bond, your name will be entered on the books of the issuer and your interest will be sent directly to you. If, however, you have purchased a bearer bond (the equivalent of holding a $1,000 bill), the dated and attached coupons must be presented to a paying agent through your bank to receive credit.

The coupon rate should not be confused with the *yield.* Yield, whether from stocks or bonds, is the rate of return received from your investment. This return on investment is key to evaluating the investment's profitability. (For a fuller explanation of return on investment on common stock, see *The Basics of Stocks,* Chapter 4.)

As a bondholder, you are faced with three kinds of yields. The first is often synonymous with the coupon if the bond was bought at par when it was issued. This yield is called the *coupon yield* or nominal yield. A new 7 percent bond with a face value of $1,000 will keep a 7 percent coupon yield for the life of the loan, since neither the principal nor the rate will change.

If you never buy anything but new bond issues at face value you will not encounter the other two kinds of yield. If, however, you buy bonds in the secondary market (the place where bonds are traded—the New York Stock Exchange, the American Stock Exchange, the over-the-counter market), you must be familiar with the *current yield* and the *yield to maturity.* Most likely, the market price you pay will not be the face value.

For example, you might have to pay 110 ($1,100) for a 7 percent bond that matures in 5 years. Since you had to pay a *premium* (a price above the face value), your 7 percent coupon gives you a current yield less than 7 percent. To figure the current yield, divide the coupon rate by the price ($70 ÷ 1,100, or 6.36 percent).

The third yield is the yield to maturity. You must take into account how the premium (or the *discount,* a price less than the face value) affects the yield when the bond is redeemed at maturity. In the above case, you paid $1,100, but will receive only $1,000 in 5 years.

The loss of $100 must be taken into account in the yield calculation. Without working out the arithmetic at this point, it is clear that the yield to maturity will be less than the coupon yield and the current yield. In fact, it is 4.76 percent.

The yield to maturity is the most critical ratio for long-term fixed-income investors. It is only the yield to maturity that considers principal, interest rate and time to redemption to arrive at the true yield.

Is your bond capable of paying your principal when it comes due? That is an important question for bondholders, and you should find out what provisions the issuer has made to pay you. You can rest easier if the corporation has a *sinking fund,* which accumulates cash needed to pay off the bond, thereby reducing the risk to the bondholder.

Finally, you should be aware of *call provisions,* which enable the bond issuer to redeem or "call" the bond earlier than the redemption date. The call provision allows the issuing corporation to save money if interest rates fall significantly below the coupon rate.

An early call will change the yield to maturity. Therefore, it is also necessary to know what the yield to the call is, should this provision be exercised.

WHY INVEST IN BONDS NOW?

After the stock market crash of October 1987, most investors found themselves wishing they had put a greater percentage of their personal holdings in fixed-income investments. The reasons for this 20/20 hindsight are obvious—bonds and money markets instruments emerged from the debacle relatively unscathed. Indeed, they even rose in price, as a massive "flight to safety" was one of the immediate consequences of the crash.

Fixed-income investments have a number of positive features that are increasingly attractive in a decreasingly stable economic environment. In the years following the meltdown, there was a decided change in American (and foreign) securities markets. Many small and individual investors in common stock reduced their equity positions. The stock markets, both here and abroad, had become more volatile than they either had expected or cared to live with.

There was also a sea change in corporate finance. Traditional ways of providing funds for companies, industries and even sovereign states, were dramatically altered. Alternate ways of financing business, extending credit and providing liquidity for corporations were developed. The way businesses raised money for their operations relied increasingly on borrowed funds (bonds) rather than equity (common stock).

New financing techniques evolved that both made it easier for companies to borrow money while they paid the lenders a higher return on their funds. One of those techniques was the development of *high-yield bonds,* which were to be used throughout the 1980s in leveraged buyouts, hostile takeovers and the restructuring of American industry.

Higher interest rates in the fixed-income market were also caused by the deregulation of the financial markets. A series of laws passed in the early 1980s removed deposit restrictions and abolished the rate limitations that had been imposed on savings institutions. Banks and savings and loan associations were free to compete for deposits by paying higher rates of interest.

The fixed-income market also became more attractive to small and individual investors by offering new instruments in smaller denominations. The new forms of debt were "user-friendly," that is, they were packaged for public consumption. For the first time, the small investor was invited into an arena that had been the playground of institutions. The bond market and fixed-interest investments had always been rather exclusive, the preserve of serious money.

Since the minimum grubstake was five or six figures ($10,000, $50,000 or $100,000), most investors paid little heed to debt instruments. They saved their money in the local bank. About the only bonds encountered were when one gave (or received) a U.S. savings bond at births, bar mitzvahs, graduations or weddings.

Once the larger investments were divided into bite-sized morsels, the public developed an appetite for bonds, baby bonds and mini-certificates that could be easily grasped. You no longer had to be wealthy to participate in the bond market.

Thus the explosion of public activity in the fixed-interest market of the '80s was directly related to the availability of smaller investments. You still needed $10,000 to buy a Treasury bill, but now you could buy a longer-term Treasury note or Treasury bond in denominations of $5,000 for maturities up to four years, and $1,000 for longer maturities. Bonds are now denominated in such small fractional parts that they are within the means of anyone who has money to invest.

Still another element helps to account for the new popularity of bonds and other debt instruments. Fluctuating interest rates also means fluctuating principal, since interest rates and principal move inversely to each other. When rates go up, the price of the security goes down, and vice versa.

A generation ago, the principle was the same, but the lower level of interest rates made the fluctuations in principal almost imperceptible, except to professional investors. However, in recent years the swings in the bond market have made it an attractive arena for *capital gains* (profit from selling assets such as a stocks or bonds).

Finally, tax changes in the 1980s made issuing bonds as well as buying bonds more attractive. Corporations were always encouraged to borrow through bond issues, since interest payments were deductible from income. Stock dividends, on the other hand, were not allowed as deductions from income. Therefore, financing through bonds did not reduce a corporation's bottom line, whereas issuing common stock did.

This tilt in favor of bonds was increased by technical changes in the tax laws, which were passed to curtail some activity in leveraged buyouts.

The Tax Reform Act of 1986 eliminated preferential tax treatment for capital gains. Capital gains from common stock were more highly valued under the old tax code, since the tax rate was at most 20 percent. With all income now taxed at the same level, there is a tendency to take certain bond income rather than uncertain capital gains.

The lure of the fixed-income market is simple: capital preservation with a reasonable return on that investment. Small investors in the stock market were perhaps the most significant victims of the 1987 crash. They left the stock market as individuals, even though the intermediaries with whom they placed some of their funds (such as banks, pension plans, profit-sharing plans and mutual funds) continued to invest in stocks. These small investors opted for greater safety in the whole range of fixed-income investments. After the crash, they took a far more serious view of how to allocate their assets.

For all these reasons, you should consider investing in the fixed-income market now. The chief concern of bond investors is preservation of capital. In these volatile times, it should be yours as well. The bond market offers the prudent investor safety and a reasonable return on money.

However, you must balance safety with growth. The key to investment success is a balanced portfolio, regardless of whether your objective is capital preservation, safety, income or growth. Remember, a total commitment to bonds will leave you exposed to price stagnation—you never get back more than your original principal (plus interest) if you are a long-term investor. And a total commitment to stocks will leave you exposed to volatility and uncertainty—you are never sure just what kind of return you will obtain on your funds.

The world of fixed-income investing is therefore certainly appropriate for balance if your portfolio consists only of common stock. It is also appropriate if all your savings are in bank accounts. Restructuring your personal assets with regard to fixed-income investments will provide you with a better equilibrium and a greater return on your money.

HOW DO BONDS BEHAVE?

Before taking a position in fixed-income investments, you should know how the market in debt obligations works. As noted, a bond is a promise to repay the purchasers the face value (usually $1,000) at a certain date in the future. The borrower promises to pay interest semiannually at the rate fixed by the coupon rate, say 7 percent ($70), or $35 every six months. When the bond is a new issue, the current yield you receive is the coupon rate, and it remains fixed as long as you hold the original issue.

Most bonds are *negotiable instruments,* that is, they can be bought and sold in the secondary market (the primary market in corporate bonds is created by the investment banking house(s) that underwrote the bond issue in the first place). However, some fixed-income instruments, such as certificates of deposit below $100,000, or U.S. savings bonds are not negotiable—they are really more like personal bank accounts.

If you wish to "sell" your non-negotiable certificate of deposit, you simply request the bank to cash it in, and the bank will credit your account (after deducting a penalty for an early withdrawal). To sell your negotiable bonds, your broker must find someone who is willing to buy them.

Most bonds are traded on the New York Stock Exchange, the American Stock Exchange or the over-the-counter market. The price at which you buy or sell is determined by supply and demand at any given moment. However, the value of bonds in the marketplace is conditioned by a number of factors.

The following are some of the more important factors determining bond prices:

- Level of prevailing interest rates
- Creditworthiness of the issuer
- Inflationary expectations
- Stages of the business cycle
- Yield

Non-negotiable fixed-income investments do not change their prices on a daily basis. Your $5,000 certificate of deposit is always worth $5,000. When it matures, its value is $5,000, plus the accumulated interest.

Negotiable bonds can change their prices every day. They are always worth their face value upon maturity.

However, they may fluctuate a great deal before they reach the end of their journey.

Interest Rates

One of the reasons for the constant change is the sensitivity of the bond market to the level of prevailing interest rates. Interest rates change fractionally throughout the day. Most of the time, the movement is not great, changing 1/32 (.031250) or 1/16 (.062500) of a bond point. (A point in the stock market is $1, but $10 in the bond market. To translate bond quotations, multiply them by 10. A quote of 92 1/2 means a dollar value of $925.)

Interest rates are in constant flux because of changing credit conditions. If the business community requires additional funds to expand operations, the cumulative demand is likely to force rates up. On the other hand, if business conditions are soft, demand for funds decreases and rates are likely to fall.

The level of interest rates is to a great degree controlled by the Federal Reserve Board. (For additional discussions on the operation of the Fed in the context of the business cycle, see *The Basics of Stocks,* Chapter 2. See also *The Basics of Investing,* Chapter 8, for an analysis of interest rates.) It does this in a number of ways, which bond investors should keep in mind, since they are clues to the direction of interest rates.

The Federal Reserve Board controls the *discount rate*— the rate at which it lends to member banks. By increasing the discount rate, it tends to make credit more costly. If it does this repeatedly, the effect will tighten the supply of money and raise rates.

The Fed also conducts the auctions of U.S. Treasury obligations. These competitive auctions determine what rates will be paid for risk-free government debt. They are key to ascertaining the direction of interest rates and the level of other money market rates, such as those offered in banks and money market funds.

The Federal Reserve Board uses other monetary tools as well. Through a number of different operations, it can alter the money supply, change credit conditions, increase or decrease bank reserves, etc.

Since the Fed rarely issues public announcements until long after it acts, the bond investor must rely on either analyzing the statistical data that is released, or follow the interpretations of an analyst who does scrutinize the Fed's elusive action. As the nation's central bank, the action of the Fed is all-important to understanding monetary events. It, however, does not readily explain its own behavior for fear of tipping off investors and speculators whose actions might be counterproductive.

If the prevailing interest rates seem destined for higher levels, the bond market will retreat. And conversely, as yields fall, bond prices will advance. The task for the bond investor is to determine whether the movements are just random fluctuations, or whether they are indeed the start of a pronounced trend.

Creditworthiness

Creditworthiness of the issuer is also factored into bond prices. Will you as a bondholder receive your interest on time, and will you get your principal back when the bond matures? In short, bondholders must be aware that there are levels of risk associated with various bonds.

Some bond issues are totally creditworthy—they contain no risk. U.S. government obligations fall into this category, as do insured bonds of municipalities.

In the corporate world, and in the field of uninsured municipal bonds, some credit risk exists. How much risk is difficult to measure with precision, since so many elements go into evaluating creditworthiness. The job has been simplified by the statistical services—they evaluate debt instruments and assign ratings.

These ratings are as carefully scrutinized by market participants as batting averages are by baseball fans. The loss or gain of a ranking is quickly translated in the marketplace to a fall or rise in a security's price. Most investment-grade bonds receive one of the four top ratings. Such bonds are considered low in risk.

For long-term investors, those who buy quality bonds and put them away to maturity, credit risk is quite low. However, there is some price risk in even the best grade of bonds.

If prevailing interest rates rise considerably above the coupon rates, the price of those bonds will fall. While this has no effect on long-term investors, short-term traders or long-term holders who are forced to sell may find that they face considerable losses.

For example, a 20-year 10 percent bond trading at par (100) $1,000 will face a decline in price if interest rates move up to 11 percent. New buyers will insist on a discount on the old 10 percent bond so that its current yield will match the new 11 percent issues. Therefore, the old bond will fall to about $909 (100 ÷ 11%).

The opposite move must also be expected should prevailing interest rates fall to 9 percent. Clearly, the old 10 percent coupon bond becomes more valuable and it will sell at a premium. The old bond will rise to about $1,111 (100 ÷ 9%) in order to have a current yield of 9 percent.

These fluctuations do not affect the long-term holder. The short-term trader may indeed welcome these fluctuations, since they provide an opportunity to profit. What should be kept in mind is that prices of negotiable bonds do fluctuate in an inverse ratio to interest rates.

This is true regardless of the bond issuer's creditworthiness. Therefore, it is possible to lose money in these conservative instruments if your object is short-term trading, or if you are forced to liquidate them before they mature.

Inflationary Expectations

While the bond market reacts immediately to changing interest rates, it also is conditioned by inflationary expectations. The fixed-income market, like the stock market, is an anticipatory mechanism. Investors continually appraise the future for signs of inflation.

Inflation is the enemy of bond prices. Higher prices (or expectation of them) mean that the purchasing power of constant dollars (such as the money locked up in bonds) will fall. This means that a 75-cent quart of milk, after a period of 5 percent inflation, will cost 96 cents in five years, the $75,000 home, $96,000.

Bond investors are sensitive to inflationary expectations and attempt to adjust prices accordingly. If increased inflation is foreseen, bond prices are likely to soften and yields rise.

Conversely, an expectation of *disinflation* (the lowering of the rate of inflation) or *deflation* (the decline of the general price level accompanied by the increase in purchasing power) will lower the yield of fixed-income investments as prices strengthen.

Business Cycle

Bond prices are also tied to the stages of the business cycle. (For a fuller explanation of the business cycle, see *The Basics of Stocks,* Chapter 2.) There are five stages to the business cycle: revival, expansion, maturation, contraction, and recession. To paraphrase an old Wall Street proverb, no one rings a bell when these stages start or end, or indeed when to buy or sell bonds.

You can use some historic precedents, however, to help make decisions about investment timing. In the revival stage, the Federal Reserve allows the money supply to expand to generate growth at the start of a new business cycle. Bond prices will continue to advance in this stage, continuing the move started earlier during the recession stage.

As the cycle accelerates and the boom continues, the Fed is likely to react to concerns about an overheated economy by cutting back on credit. The *federal funds* rate (the overnight lending rate among banks) and the discount rate are increased. At the first signs of this tightening of credit, short-term and intermediate-term bondholders should consider selling, since bond prices are likely to soften as yields rise.

In the advanced stage of the business cycle, maturation, all but long-term holders should be out of the bond market. Prices retreat in the face of expected inflation, a feature that accompanies the end of a business boom. The Fed has applied the brakes by continuing to raise short-term rates.

Bond prices continue to fall throughout the economic contraction as business declines. Bond buyers are now on the sidelines, or in short-term money market instruments.

Finally, the last stage, recession, is again an appropriate time to buy bonds. Business conditions range between weak to awful. Credit is not in demand. Bond prices are low, and yields are high, both on money market funds and intermediate or long-term bonds. When the Federal Reserve starts to stimulate the economy to recover, bonds will perk up, giving you both high yield and capital appreciation if you are astute enough to buy them when no one else wants them.

By using the business cycle, you can remove some of the guesswork from investment decisions. But bear in mind that the classic business cycle has also undergone some change. In recent years, the economy has experienced rolling recessions and rolling recoveries, affecting different parts of the economy at different times. It has become difficult to identify the beginning and end of the various stages of the business cycle.

Whether a short-term or long-term investor, you should be able to buy and sell bonds easily and without any price concessions. There are thousands of bond issues, but not all of them are tradable. Many small issues lack liquidity—there is virtually no market for the $6 million issue of New Jersey Hackensack Water 10s of 2,000; on the other hand, the $500 million issue of AT&T 8.80s of 2,000 can be bought and sold immediately.

Liquidity is simply the ability to turn your fixed-income investment into cash quickly, without taking a significant loss because there are hardly any buyers. You can avoid a liquidity trap (you never know when you will have to liquidate an asset in an emergency) by buying only government bonds or issues of well-known corporations or municipalities.

Special exotic issues may have some advantages in yield, price or other benefits, but these issues are best left to professional investors who are better able to cope with the special conditions.

Yield

This is perhaps the chief consideration in bond pricing. Since it is so important, the next chapter is devoted to it.

Y · O · U · R   M · O · V · E

- Consider the advantages of fixed-income investments. Would additional income be welcomed in your present circumstances? Are your retirement plans taking into account the benefits of bonds?
- How did you emerge from the crash of 1987? If you had had more of your assets in fixed-income investments would you be in better shape now?
- You never thought about the bond market, since you suspected that mega-dollars were needed to participate. Since there are now a variety of fixed-income investments in small denominations, perhaps it is time to reconsider this market.
- All your savings are in various bank deposits. Have you taken into account that the fixed-income market pays a higher return on your money? Are you aware that there are a number of instruments whose principal and interest are guaranteed so that they are as safe as bank deposits?
- Be sure that you understand the key relationship in the bond market: when interest rates rise, principal falls, and vice versa. This seesaw ratio dominates the world of negotiable bonds. Liquidity, inflation, creditworthiness, business cycles and yield all play a role in pricing bonds, but the movement of interest rates is perhaps the most important item to keep in mind.

• 2 •

Figuring Bond Yields

WHICH YIELD IS RIGHT FOR YOU?

Most investors in fixed-income investments are primarily interested in how much more money they can make on their original money. For long-term investors, this *return on investment* comes largely from the interest paid by the debt obligations. For short-term traders, some of the return on investment will come from interest, but some will also be derived from capital gains.

There is, of course, no way of knowing beforehand what rate of return traders will make on the assets they control. However, the yield on fixed-income investments for long-term investors is relatively predictable, especially if they are held to maturity.

The rate of return on an asset (whether a bond, certificate of deposit or other debt instrument) is equal to the income yielded as a percentage of the asset's value. In other words, a $1,000 bond (bought at face value) pays $70 of interest, a 7 percent return on investment.

For long-term buyers holding the bond to maturity, they will receive 7 percent every year—the return on investment will not change. For the short-term trader who sells at the end of year, the return on investment depends on the sale price. Three results are possible: If the bond is sold at the price it was bought, $1,000, the rate of return remains at 7 percent. If interest rates rose and the price of the bond fell to $900, the return would be minus 3 percent. If interest rates fell and the price of the bond rose to $1,100, the return would be 17 percent.

Simple versus Compound Interest

What makes the picture more complicated is the fact that, while many people spend their interest income as it is paid, many do not. The recent popularity of *mortgage-backed securities* (certificates issued by U.S. government agencies representing an interest in a large pool of home mortgages) rests on their relatively high yields, but also on their provisions for paying interest and principal on a monthly basis. Individuals looking for steady income, especially on a monthly basis, are not concerned about earning interest on their interest.

Nevertheless, many investors seek to make money on the money they have already earned. The simple interest paid by many debt obligations makes no provision for the earned interest. It makes no difference whether the bond was bought at par, at a premium, or at a discount—the interest earned is *simple interest.*

To be perfectly clear, a brief review of the difference between simple and *compound interest* will show you the benefits of the latter.

To calculate simple interest, you must know three things: the principal, the rate of interest and the time or duration that the money is lent or borrowed. The basic formula is:

Interest = Principal × Rate of interest × Time

For further information, see "The Arithmetic of Interest Rates," a booklet written by Richard D. C. Trainer and published by the Federal Reserve Bank of New York. The booklet may be obtained free of charge from the Federal Reserve Bank, 33 Liberty Street, New York, NY 10045.

Most people and financial organizations demand compound interest. The three same elements of principal, rate and time are used, but this formula is slightly more complicated:

$$F = P \ (1 + R)^T$$

In this equation, F is the total repayment, or the principal plus the total accumulated interest; P is the principal; R is the rate of interest; and T is the time, in years.

It is possible to compound more than annually—multiple compounding could be semiannually, quarterly, monthly or even daily. Certificates of deposits of banks have no consistent policy, ranging from simple interest to virtually continuous compounding.

In Table 2.1, you can see the advantage of compounding daily or compounding annually over earning simple interest for $1,000 at 7 percent.

Bondholders who reinvest their interest payments rather than spend them can then obtain interest on their interest, or compound interest. For the bondholder, this is the best possible alternative, especially if the reinvestment can be done at higher rates than the original coupon rate. The return on investment in this case is called the *total rate of return*.

Three Kinds of Yields

There are a number of ways to express yield. If you can appreciate the differences, then you will be able to apply the right yield measurement for your needs. There are three kinds of yields:

TABLE 2.1   Advantage of Compounding Daily or Annually over
Simple Interest

No. of Years	Simple Interest	Compounded Annually	Compounded Daily
1	$1,070	$1,070	$1,074
2	1,070	1,145	1,153
3	1,070	1,225	1,237
4	1,070	1,311	1,328
5	1,070	1,403	1,426

Calculations based on $1,000 invested at 7 percent interest.

1. The coupon yield
2. The current yield
3. The yield to maturity

The *coupon yield* is the stated rate of interest that a fixed-income investment will pay on a regular basis over the term of its life. Once that rate is fixed in the *bond indenture*, the formal contract between the borrower and the trustee representing the lenders, it will remain unchanged.

If a $1,000 face value bond agrees to pay 7.5 percent ($75) a year, then the coupon yield is 7.5 percent. Anyone who purchases the bond originally or who buys it later on at face value in the secondary market will receive the coupon yield of 7.5 percent.

When bonds are bought in the secondary market, the usual price is anything but its face value. Whether you buy a bond above par (at a premium) or below (at a discount), you must know what the current yield is to be sure that it compares favorably with other comparable investments.

Should the 7.5 percent bond sell at par in the secondary market, the current yield would be the same as the coupon yield. More likely, however, is that the bond will be selling at a premium in a low interest environment or at a discount in a high one.

To calculate the current yield, divide the coupon rate by the purchase price:

$$\frac{\text{Coupon rate}}{\text{Purchase price}} = \text{Current yield}$$

If you purchase a $1,000 face value 7.5 percent bond at a premium of 110 (or $1,100):

$$\frac{\$75}{\$1,100} = 6.82\%$$

When purchased at a discount of 90 (or $900):

$$\frac{\$75}{\$900} = 8.33\%$$

As a rule, bonds selling at a premium have a lower current yield than the coupon rate. Bonds selling at a discount have a higher current yield than the coupon rate. You must decide how the bonds under consideration compare with what else is in the marketplace. How does the current yield stack up to the yields reported in the financial press?

As noted earlier, the *prevailing interest rates* determine the day-to-day movement of fixed-income prices. Interest rates are, of course, different for every category of money (See Table 2.2). Therefore, you must consult the tables published in the daily newspapers or weekly periodicals to see those current rates.

In addition, there are other tables indicating the yields on municipal bonds, corporate securities, mortgage securities, etc. By reading these key tables, you will immediately

TABLE 2.2 Sample Money Rates (Percentages)

	Yesterday	Previous Day	Year Ago
Prime rate	8.50	8.50	10.50
Discount	5.00	5.50	7.00
3-mo. Treas. bills	5.45	5.50	7.66
6-mo. Treas. bills	5.54	5.63	7.73
7-yr. Treas. notes	7.30	7.35	8.48
30-yr. Treas. bonds	8.06	8.08	8.97
Certificates of deposit			
180 days	5.39	5.42	7.49
Money market accounts	5.00	5.01	5.89
Money market funds	5.34	5.37	7.57
Corporate bonds			
AAA Industrials	8.56	8.56	9.37

see the current yields offered so that you can make comparisons.

You would not pay the face value for an already issued 7.5 percent bond when you can buy a new one of comparable quality with a coupon yield of 8.5 percent, a reflection of current interest rate levels. To be competitive, the older issue must trade down, that is, its price must fall so that its current yield will be equal to the new coupon rate of 8.5 percent. In order to do that, the price has to fall to about $882—at that level, it offers a current yield of 8.5 percent, equivalent to the new issue.

If the prevailing interest rates plunge to 6.5 percent, then the 7.5 percent bond would clearly be a good buy if you are looking for higher current income. But the market is a continually adjusting mechanism so that as current rates fall, the price of higher coupon bonds rises. Thus the 7.5 percent bond would move to a premium of about $1,152, where the current yield would equal 6.5 percent.

The third type of yield, the *yield to maturity,* is the one calculated over time. It is not enough to know the coupon yield and the current yield: you also need to know the return on your funds to the time that the bond matures.

To calculate yield to maturity, you must realize that, generally speaking, all issues come back to *par* (their face value, which is usually $1,000) when they are redeemed. If you have paid a premium (a purchase price over par) for a high-yielding bond, you will lose that premium by maturity. If you bought the bond at a discount, you can consider the difference between the discount price and the face value as additional yield.

Calculating a precise yield to maturity is not necessary, since every brokerage house and bank has tables of values. In fact, some financial publications list in their bond tables the yield to maturity in their columns of statistical information.

Since yield to maturity is a common denominator, all bonds tend to be quoted on that basis. The point to remember is that yield to maturity represents the total present value of all coupon payments until redemption, plus the present value of the face amount of the bond at the maturity date.

Or to put it slightly differently, the yield to maturity is the discount rate in a present value calculation, which makes all cash payments over the bond's remaining life (coupon payments and principal) equal to the bond's market value.

What is clear from the yield to maturity is that even though a premium bond has a higher current yield, the discount bond may have a higher yield to maturity.

You must decide which is more important—high current income now, or high income later. If you want high current income, you might buy a premium bond, since it is at a premium because it does have a desirable coupon rate. Conversely, you might buy a discounted bond which would lower current income (and presumably taxes) but produce larger future gains.

(For a detailed explanation of yield to maturity, see Appendix A.)

WHAT IS THE TOTAL RETURN?

While yield to maturity is a critical measurement for anyone buying bonds, it does not tell the whole story. One of the problems with fixed-income investments is that the total return of funds over time depends not only on the yield to maturity, but on what is done with the semiannual interest payments.

A great difference exists between spending the interest as it is paid, saving the interest in a savings account or reinvesting the interest at a comparable or higher rate. Your personal circumstances will of course dictate the answer: Many people live off these interest payments. However, if you do not, you should be aware of the benefits of compounding.

A bond may continue to yield 8 percent for the rest of its life, as is the nature of quality bonds, but you will not have a true 8 percent yield unless the semiannual interest payments also obtain 8 percent. That, however, is difficult to ensure, since a new economic environment is likely to bring higher or lower rates, rarely the same as the coupon rate of the original issue.

While yield to maturity can be calculated in a bond with certainty, the same is not true for your total return, since there is no way of predicting at what rate you will be able to invest the periodic interest payments. If your reinvestment rate is lower than the yield to maturity, your rate of return will be less, while if it is higher your total return will exceed the yield to maturity.

This problem of the reinvestment rate, or what to do with interest, is one of the great questions in the fixed-income world. The only partial solution is to buy *zero coupon bonds* (bonds that pay no periodic interest but grow in value at a fixed rate) or *original issue deep discount bonds* (bonds that are issued at a discount and with a low coupon rate). These bonds may fluctuate a great deal in price, but the eventual true return on capital is predictable. The true return and yield to maturity are then the same.

The solution is only partial, since you lose the option of investing in higher yields when (and if) they come along. Once you've locked yourself into a long-term zero or deep discounted bond, the bonds will go down when the prevailing yield goes up. The market action of these kinds of securities is more volatile than for instruments that pay full interest on a regular basis. So while they guarantee a fixed rate of return when held to redemption, they do fluctuate a great deal.

Consequently, taking advantage of the best yields is no easy matter, and jumping in and out of bonds is ill-advised for anyone but the professional. Since you will never be able to receive the best rates at all times, the answer is to diversify, both as to maturities and as to purchases.

Few nonprofessionals exhibit enough diligence or foresight to "ride the yield curve," that is, to transact trades that continually produce the highest returns on funds. This can usually be accomplished on a normal sloping yield curve by buying long maturities, holding them for a while, then swapping them for shorter maturities to eke out the interest rate differentials. It is not a recommended strategy for anyone not in the business. However, swapping bonds does have a worthwhile place in reducing income taxes if you have a capital loss on your bonds.

ALL YIELDS ARE NOT CREATED EQUAL

For reasons too elaborate to explain here, yields from different fixed-income investments, savings accounts, certificates of deposit and Treasury paper are not always comparable. In general, *yield* means the rate of return on your investment, most commonly expressed in terms of percent per year. As we saw, yield in a savings bank is sometimes calculated as simple interest. Certificates of deposit and time deposits in most banks are based on compound interest—thus they advertise both the interest rate and the yield, which reflects the compounding.

Banks do not use a calendar year of 365 days, but a commercial year of 360 days. To find the equivalent of what banks term the *CD basis*, that is, to determine the true yearly interest rate, it is necessary to convert:

$$\frac{\text{Interest rate or coupon rate} \times \text{Principal}}{\text{Commercial year}} = \text{Daily interest}$$

Thus, for an 8 percent yield on a $10,000 face-value bond invested for one year,

$$\frac{.08 \times 10,000}{360} = \$2.22$$

Thus a deposit for a year would not yield $800, but $811.03, or 8.11 percent of simple interest per year. A shortcut formula is:

$$\text{Interest rate or coupon rate} \times \frac{\text{Calendar year}}{\text{Commercial year}}$$

$$\frac{.08 \times 365}{360} = 8.11\%$$

Some banks use a CD or 360-day basis, but some banks quote an equivalent bond yield, which means that a year deposit will earn interest at the stated rate for 365 days. Bond equivalent yields are always higher, since you are being paid interest over a somewhat longer period. The difference is fractional, but you should know which basis your interest rate is being quoted.

The following is a simple table of equivalents so that you can check the difference:

Yield on Bank CD or Discount Basis	*Equivalent Bond Yield One-Year Maturity*
5.00	5.34
6.00	6.48
7.00	7.64
8.00	8.82
9.00	10.04
10.00	11.28

Bonds state a coupon rate—the interest rate is not compounded. The yield on bonds can be slightly greater for the year if the semiannual interest payment is reinvested for the next six months. Thus, an 8 percent coupon can have a higher return if the $40 is put to work at 8 percent ($3.20 per year or $1.60 for six months): The $40 from the first six months will become $41.60, plus the $40 from the second six-month period—for a total of $81.60, or 8.16 percent.

Bonds are interest-bearing long-term securities. As a general rule, they quote interest earned on a 365-day basis. Short-term bonds, however, usually pay interest on a discounted basis.

Treasury bills (which mature in 13, 26 or 52 weeks) are sold on a discounted basis. You send the Treasury a minimum of $10,000 before the auction. (If you buy the bill directly from the Federal Reserve Bank, you will save the modest charges imposed by brokerage houses and commercial banks.) Individuals tender their bids on a non-competitive basis.

There is no coupon rate, just a discount from par. In other words, the bills are sold at a discount and later redeemed at face value. Once the auction has established the price (the private investor receives an average price determined by the auction), you receive a check from the Federal Reserve Bank within a week.

The check represents the difference between the purchase price and the face value of the Treasury bill at maturity. This difference between what you pay and what you receive, the discount, is the interest payment.

If the bid was for only 13 weeks, the return discount would be a quarter of the full discount. If the auction sets the price at 92 ($9,200), the buyer of the one-year bill will receive an $800 check—an 8 percent discount. But the actual yield is slightly more, since an investment of $9,200 is returning $800 ($800 ÷ $9,200) or 8.70 percent.

The buyer now has $800 to invest. If it is invested at 8 percent, the investor has an additional $64. The return of $64, plus the $800, produces a yield of ($864 ÷ $10,000) 8.64 percent for the $10,000. Furthermore, Treasury bill interest is free of state and local income taxes, so the after-tax yield is even higher.

THE YIELD CURVE AND
INTEREST RATES

For a long time in American history, interest rates were low and constant (except for an occasional money panic). A 3 percent interest rate was considered a fair return on one's funds in periods when inflation was absent.

Since the mid-1970s, that situation dramatically changed, as growing inflationary trends stimulated a rise in interest rates. Global inflation started with the Vietnam war and accelerated with the OPEC oil embargo in 1974. Since then, rates of inflation have been as high as 14 percent in 1979 and as low as 3 percent in 1981.

In recent years, investors and consumers have become more conscious of interest rate levels as they rapidly rose and fell. Higher rates meant additional family expenses, but they also have meant additional income. So all investors and lenders of funds must ask themselves these questions: What are realistic interest rates for my funds? How do I protect the future purchasing power of the money I invest?

Some investors look back at the old 3 percent rule as a useful abstraction. The rate of return on their money should equal the prevailing inflation rate plus the 3 percent that money has historically earned. As a rough guide, this rule has much validity.

For example, the average rate of 3-month Treasury bills (an indication of short-term interest rates) from 1976 through 1989 was about 9.50 percent, while the average consumer price index (a measurement of inflation) for the same period was 6.35 percent—a difference of 3.15 percent. Short-term investors were obtaining that historic 3 percent differential for their funds.

Historic precedent aside, you can see what level of interest rates the money markets are now paying by looking at what is known as the *yield curve*. The yield curve is a graphic display showing the rates presently being paid for money over all periods of time, from a few months to 30 or more years. It is a distillation of the total supply and demand for funds at every maturity. It is also by its nature a distillation of all the known economic, financial and political considerations about money, both now and in the foreseeable future.

There are many different types of yield curves—one for every category of security. But the most prominent is the one for Treasury securities, since it reflects the true interest rate for virtually risk-free money. It is a measurement of the safest lending—lending to the U.S. government. To put it a little differently, the Treasury yield curve is a floor for interest rates.

The normal yield curve is a continuous line, positively sloped with short-term rates lower than long-term rates (Figure 2.1).

This normal curve is a reflection of reasonably stable conditions. There are ample funds to borrow and an adequate supply of debt instruments. The short end of the range (3 months to 1 year) reflects the rates available to lenders who wish to remain *liquid* while waiting for a clearer picture of the investment scene. (Liquidity has a special meaning here: the desire not to commit one's funds to longer maturities. However, the Treasury market is extremely liquid, in that purchases and sales of Treasury securities can be transacted immediately.)

The short end of the Treasury market is greatly influenced by the Federal Reserve Board's monetary action. The ratcheting of the discount rate, adjusting the federal funds rate, the actions of the open market committee, stabilizing the dollar, tuning the money supply and manipulating the Treasury auctions all give the Fed great power to influence short-term interest rates.

The yield curve can be subjected to specific events that cause it to react to demand for government obligations. A so-called "flight to quality" can alter the supply-demand balance as investors sell higher-risk, nongovernment securities because of some momentous event to hunker down with Treasury securities.

The medium-term range (one year to ten years) is less volatile and is used by investors for fixed goals, especially in the four-year and seven-year category. This plateau or

FIGURE 2.1   Normal Yield Curve

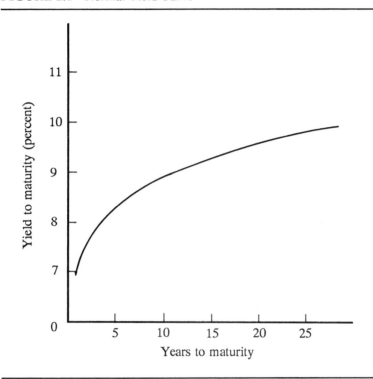

"hump" is often the sweet spot for investors, since it gives the best yields without having to tie money up for the long term.

Long-term bonds (ten to 30 years) are the arena for institutional investors, insurance companies, pension funds and organizations that must fix their returns over long periods. Institutions need the predictability of the long-term bond market so that they can calculate their returns on investments to satisfy claims of annuitants, pensioners and depositors in future years.

The yield curve is not always normal, that is, a gradually sloped rise from the short to the long end. Occasion-

FIGURE 2.2   Inverted Yield Curve

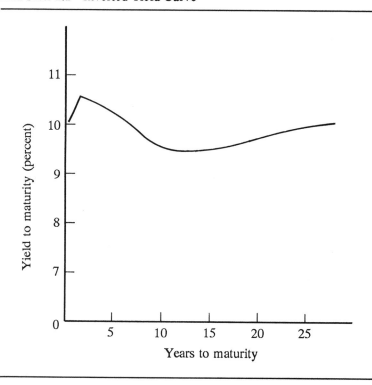

Years to maturity

ally, the curve inverts, and short-term interest rates rise above long ones (Figure 2.2).

An inverted yield curve usually results when the Fed tightens the availability of credit. For example, as a consequence of fear about inflation and an overheated economy, Treasury bills (due in one year) now yield more than Treasury notes (due in ten years).

Short-term rates rise as businesses scramble to borrow now, believing conditions will worsen tomorrow. This, of course, becomes a self-fulfilling prophesy. As companies find it more expensive to maintain inventories, they cut back on production, workers are laid off and manufacturers reduce their orders for raw materials and parts. When the Fed tightens credit too long or too much, a recession results.

It is tempting to conclude that an inverted yield curve is a clue to a coming recession. However, a study of inversions by Charles Lieberman, the director of research for the old Manufacturers Hanover Bank (now Chemical Bank), found that while a recession is always preceded by a yield curve inversion, a recession does not automatically follow every yield curve inversion.

Given a normal yield curve, bond investors tend to be comfortable with short-term rates. However, as they look out further, a host of questions—how much inflation, how will the government deal with the deficits, will we enter a protectionist war with our trading partners—make them unsure. Hence, long-term bonds require higher rates of interest to overcome lenders' reluctance to commit their funds.

Given an inverted yield curve, investor psychology changes because of active Fed intervention and uncertain government policies. Since economic conditions are unstable and a recession threatens, lenders will not make long-term loans and can only be induced to make short-term ones at increasingly higher levels.

In short, if investors think interest rates are going up, they will stay with short maturities to avoid being locked in with long, low-yielding ones. On the other hand, borrowers wish to obtain cheap funds as long as possible and try to extend maturities. Both actions make for a normal, upward-sloping yield curve.

But when interest rates are perceived to be going down, lenders then buy long-term bonds in the effort to lock in high yields. Borrowers naturally take the opposite view and set extremely high short-term rates so that they can refinance their debt a little later at lower levels. Both actions help produce the inverted yield curve.

The yield curve determines the price of money—the interest rate. Normally, it arcs upward, showing that short-term rates are only fractionally higher than present rates. As you move away in time, the curve rises and the interest rate increases in the medium-term range. Finally, it plateaus somewhere between the medium and long-term range. The Treasury yield curve changes virtually every day, but it is one of the most important sources of market information regarding what interest rates are expected to do in the short-term and long-term.

For the fixed-income investor, the graphic display of the yield curve in the financial press is one of the most important indicators of interest rates. Most publications present you with not only the current yield curve but one that represents rates from last week, last month or a year ago. You can then compare rates and make a determination as to which maturities and yields are most advantageous.

Y · O · U · R   M · O · V · E

- Before buying fixed-income investments, make sure your objectives are clear. Know when you want the funds to be free so that you can be precise about maturity dates. For college funds or retirement accounts, consider staggered maturities for an even cash flow.
- Find all three critical yields (coupon, current and yield to maturity) so that you can calculate how much money your funds are earning, especially if you are buying bonds in the secondary market.
- If you want a maximum return, then you need a high coupon and you may have to pay a premium. But if you wish a high yield at maturity, the current yield can be relatively low and you should look at discounted bonds

with low coupons that will appreciate as they move to call or redemption.

- Understand whether your funds are earning simple or compound interest. Compound interest is better, since yields are higher in time deposits such as CDs, but you may also be penalized if you try to move to higher rates in the following years. Bond interest is simple interest, leaving you with the problem of reinvesting the earned interest. Your total return is based on what you do with the accumulated interest.

- It is better to lock in high yields for a long maturity, but it can be profitable to leave 20 to 30 percent of the portfolio for the short end of the market to take advantage of inverted yield curves. When the curve inverts, consider buying short-term paper not only for the highest yields, but for liquidity and safety, since an inversion means that a recession may well be around the corner.

- Inordinately high yields are signs of weakness rather than strength. High-yielding bonds should be used only to elevate yield in the attic, not build the foundation in the basement. No more than 10 percent of your portfolio should be in speculative issues. The one sure road to disaster in a fixed income portfolio is over-reaching. If the yield is out of line with the yield curve, someone knows something you don't—and what is known is depressing the value of the investment and raising its return.

• 3 •

Risk-Free Fixed-Income Investments Without Fluctuations

WHAT YOU SEE IS WHAT YOU GET

The selection of fixed-income investments is vast. There is now something for everyone's taste, from the most prudent to the most adventuresome. However, investors generally consider fixed-income assets to be safer than common stock. It is more advantageous to be owed money and be paid interest than to own a fractional share in a business.

Risk is perhaps the foremost consideration for fixed-income investors. While the overwhelming majority of fixed-income investments are safe and secure, in recent years the financial world has witnessed the creation of some debt obligations that are every bit as risky as penny stocks.

Moreover, financial conditions of corporations now change so rapidly because of takeovers, buyouts, mergers and acquisitions that high-quality investment grade bonds can be occasionally turned into speculative investments overnight.

The active fixed-income investor must not only invest prudently but constantly monitor that portion of your portfolio exposed to market risk.

If you wish to avoid risk completely, yet partake in the higher returns available to fixed-income investments, you should consider four types of investments: money market accounts, money market funds, certificates of deposit and U.S. savings bonds. These investments allow you to recapture your principal completely without being subject to the ups and downs of interest-rate fluctuations associated with the bond market.

MONEY MARKET ACCOUNTS

Description

To compete with the highly successful money market funds, which were introduced in the early 1970s, banks as well as savings and loan associations began to offer money market accounts in the early 1980s after financial deregulation was phased in.

Since the accounts are offered within the banking structure, deposits are guaranteed under FDIC up to $100,000. This is the major difference between money market accounts and money market funds. Interest rates are set by the banks and are based not only on the cost of their funds but on competitive circumstances as well. Rates are not adjusted as frequently as with the funds.

Risk and Return

With the federal government's guarantee of these money market accounts, there is clearly no risk if the bank is insured (not all banks are so insured, however.) Money market accounts are not rated by rating services, but the banks are themselves rated. Considering that between 100 and 200 banks fail every year, look for a bank with a favorable rating and save yourself possible trouble.

Remember, the banks that offer the highest rates are frequently the ones that are on the shakiest ground.

Maturity and Duration

Money market accounts are a form of demand deposit; as such, they have no maturity dates. As long as the account remains active, interest will be paid. While typically a minimum deposit is required to establish such an account and the number of withdrawals that are allowed in a month is limited, anyone with a savings account should consider switching to a money market account at the very same teller's window. Federal Reserve studies show that billions of dollars are eligible for higher rates.

Income and Yield

Initially, money market accounts paid more than money market funds to lure new depositors. But in recent years, their rate of return has fallen below that of money market funds. Because the federal guarantee issued by the Federal Deposit Insurance Corporation (FDIC) is persuasive to some who might otherwise use money market funds, the banks take advantage of that perception and tend to pay lower yields than the money market funds offer.

For instance, at the end of 1991 bank money market accounts were paying 4.5 percent, as reported by the *Bank Rate Monitor*, while money market funds were paying an average 4.7 percent, according to Donoghue's *Money Fund Report*. The banks impose no transaction costs for opening these accounts, but they may also drop the interest rate if the principal amount falls below a given level.

Special Benefits

Money market accounts offer no special tax benefit. The earned interest is fully taxable as income.

MONEY MARKET FUNDS

Description

Since the early 1970s, when money market funds were first introduced, these vehicles have won a huge following. More than 400 of these funds manage close to half a trillion dollars. These funds are *mutual funds* (investment companies that stand ready to buy and sell their shares at the net asset value of their underlying portfolio holdings), but they are composed not of stocks, but a variety of quality debt instruments: Treasury bills, certificates of deposit, commercial paper and bankers' acceptances.

All these obligations have short life spans: they mature within 30 or 60 days. This enables the funds to earn interest at the current or prevailing rates as they constantly turn over their portfolios. This also means that interest rates constantly change from week to week. Investors purchase a fractional share of the underlying portfolio's net asset value. Each share of the fund is priced at $1.

After an initial purchase (the minimum is usually $500 or $1,000, depending on the fund), an investor can buy any amount. The value of the shares always remains fixed at $1. Interest is credited by way of issuing additional shares. The price of the shares never changes, but the number of shares increases in proportion to the amount of interest earned. The money market funds allow small investors to obtain the same yields as were previously reserved for institutions and the wealthy.

Risk and Rating

Money market funds have proven to be safe since their inception, but the principal is (with but one or two exceptions) not guaranteed by the federal government or private insurance. The diverse nature of their portfolios plus the superior quality of their holdings and their short maturities reduces the risk enormously. If you want to have your money market investment guaranteed, choose money market funds that limit their portfolios to Treasury securities.

The rating agencies do rank money market funds. There is a great similarity among the funds.

Maturity and Duration

Money market funds are a form of demand account: you either receive a book of checks or you can telephone for a check to be issued. In many funds a minimum has been established for deposits and withdrawals. These funds are not meant for daily check-clearing activity. Originally, these funds were thought of as temporary havens where one could park money while waiting for further investment possibilities. However, many investors have found that they are excellent vehicles for achieving the highest immediate yields combined with instant liquidity without being subject to a withdrawal fee or interest penalty.

Income and Yield

While money market funds return among the highest current yields, the yields change constantly. You may receive 6 percent at the beginning of the year and only 4.5 percent at the end of the year, or vice versa. The funds offer no yield guarantees, nor do they lock in an interest rate. They do, however, closely reflect the rates decided on by the weekly Treasury auctions. Since there are no transaction costs or commission fees and only a relatively small management fee, the yields of money market funds truly reflect the return available to the largest investors without any governmental limitations or controls. Money market funds usually yield .25 to .50 percent more than short-term Treasury bills. There are also special purpose funds, such as the previously mentioned one based on government securities. Tax-exempt money market funds pay considerably less than the taxable funds, somewhere between 70 and 90 percent of Treasury bills. In the beginning of 1980 money market funds were yielding almost 14 percent. In 1991 they were returning less than 5 percent.

Special Benefits

In general, money market funds offer no special tax benefits. However, there are various tax-free money market funds which invest only in the tax-free obligations of those states. The interest from those funds is naturally tax-free.

CERTIFICATES OF DEPOSIT

Description

Certificates of deposit (CDs) are issued by banks and thrifts (savings and loan associations) in return for funds deposited with them for a specified amount of time. CDs come in a variety of denominations: the most popular start at $500 and end with jumbos of $100,000. These CDs are nonnegotiable receipts. Some are simply book-entry notations on a bank or brokerage statement.

Some banks offer larger CDs (of $1 million and up) to institutional investors. These are negotiable instruments and they are actively traded. In recent years, large brokerage houses have entered the small CD market to act as clearing houses. They use their national presence to scour the country for the best rates, which they then make available to their clients. But they also provide an additional service by selling the CDs before they mature. This enables clients to unload CDs in a secondary market without incurring the usual penalty associated with CDs purchased from the bank. In addition, the brokerage house analysts review what is offered, thereby filtering out the most dubious offerings.

Risk and Rating

The FDIC insures CD accounts in banks and thrifts up to $100,000. This federal insurance agency places the full faith and credit of the U.S. government behind these deposits. Not all banks participate in this federal program; some are insured by state governments. The crisis in state-insured banks a few years ago has improved coverage, but the prudent investor will opt for federal protection.

With the banks and thrifts under considerable financial pressure from bad loans, mismanagement and fraud, you will save yourself time and trouble by buying CDs from deposit institutions with investment-grade ratings.

Maturity and Duration

Certificates of deposit typically mature in as little as six months or as much as five years. Some meet specific maturity dates instead of fixed periods. If you cash in a CD before its due date, you stand to lose between three and six months' worth of interest.

Income and Yield

CDs earn interest in different ways, depending on the bank's accounting procedures. There are half a dozen ways to calculate interest, from simple interest once a year to continuous compounding on a daily basis. The differences can be significant, especially when large sums are under consideration. The more frequently the principal is compounded, the faster interest accrues and the higher the return. All CDs have a *nominal* rate, that is, the stated rate of interest paid. They also have an *effective yield,* the actual rate arising from the compounding of the principal and accumulating interest. Thus the two figures are advertised in bank windows and in the media, the latter always more than the former.

To determine the yield on a bank CD, you must calculate the daily interest rate:

$$\frac{\text{Interest rate}}{360\,\text{days}} \times \text{Principal} = \text{Daily interest rate}$$

Thus an 8 percent CD for $5,000 has a daily interest rate of:

$$\frac{.08}{360} \times \$5,000 = \$1.111$$

Banks use a 360-day basis for their accounting. If the daily interest is multiplied by 365 days, the total is $405.52, and the annual rate of simple interest ($405.52 ÷ $5,000) is 8.11 percent.

Special Benefits

CDs have no special tax advantage unless they are deposited in a tax-advantaged account (such as an individual retirement account [IRA] or a self-employed retirement plan).

U.S. SAVINGS BONDS

Description

U.S. savings bonds are one of the most common investments, no doubt because they are guaranteed by the federal government. Another reason for their popularity is their availability: they come in small denominations starting with face values of $50 and $100, and ending with $10,000. Anyone can buy up to $30,000 worth (face value) a year. A major drawback to these bonds is that they are not negotiable.

Risk and Rating

There is virtually no credit risk with U.S. savings bonds, since these U.S. obligations have always been redeemed. Consequently, they are not rated by the financial services.

Maturity and Duration

These bonds *mature* in ten years, that is, they reach their full face value at that time. However, though not negotiable, it is possible to redeem them at any time after their initial six-month period.

Income and Yield

The purchase price for EE series savings bonds (the only series now available to the public) is half the face value. The EE series pays only 4.16 percent for the first five years and then a minimum of 6 percent for the remaining five years. The government adjusts this rate from time to time; until late 1986 the rate was 7.5 percent. To make these bonds more attractive, the Treasury has increased the potential yield by tying the rate of return to the average yield on 5-year Treasury notes. You will receive 85 percent of the average Treasury note yield—the interest rate is set twice a year, in May and November. The investor is guaranteed a minimum rate of 6 percent but will obtain a higher rate if the market so dictates. You do not pay a fee or commission when you buy or redeem U.S. savings bonds.

Special Benefits

U.S. savings bonds are free of city and state taxes. They have an additional bonus: Once they mature after ten years, they can be rolled over (tax-free) into series HH bonds (with a minimum $500 denomination). This series pays interest at a straight 6 percent on a semiannual basis. The interest is taxable on a current year basis, but the gain from the EE series accumulation is not taxable until the HH bonds are redeemed. Finally, savings bonds that are used to pay for college tuition are tax-free.

Y • O • U • R   M • O • V • E

- Fixed-income, nonfluctuating investments are suitable for you if you would like to receive higher returns on your funds, but dislike the notion of the principal increasing or decreasing in value in response to changes in interest rates.
- Fixed-income, nonfluctuating investments are also suitable for you if you are not quite sure when you will need the invested funds. There may indeed be a small penalty for liquidating CDs or U.S. savings bonds (which amounts to a slightly lower rate of interest), but your original investment always remains intact.
- Decide as best you can when you will need the funds. The longer investment period usually obtains the best interest rates. If your horizon is three to five years, you are likely to find the best rates in certificates of deposit. If your horizon is longer than five years, U.S. savings bonds guarantee a reasonable rate of return, with a sweetener of a higher return should Treasury interest rates increase.

- Money market funds are temporary shelters for investment funds. Rates fluctuate from week to week, so there is no predictability of interest earnings. You can shop for the best rates by consulting the financial newspapers for national comparisons.
- Money market accounts in banks are insured, but they are likely to yield the lowest rates of all the nonfluctuating, fixed-income investments. On the other hand, they provide you with safety and the convenience of your local bank.

• 4 •

U.S. Governments: Risk-Free Investments with Fluctuations

U.S. TREASURY BILLS

The largest and safest investment market in the world is that of U.S. Treasury securities, especially Treasury bills. The U.S. Treasury issues billions of dollars of obligations each year to cover federal expenditures and deficits. Approximately 40 percent of all that debt is issued in the form of short-term, negotiable, non-interest bearing securities, better known as T-bills. In the market for government securities, 50 percent of the trading involves T-bills—over $100 billion every day.

Treasury bills have the complete backing of the government—known as a "full faith and credit" pledge. The U.S. has never defaulted on its loans, and investors can have total confidence that their funds will be paid back. Investors around the world regard T-bills as the equivalent of cash.

However, they do fluctuate in price to some degree. Since they are short-term instruments, that fluctuation is likely to be small as they move toward maturity. If you buy Treasury bills, you are more than likely to receive back your original investment if you are obliged to sell them before they are redeemed.

Description

U.S. Treasury bills consist of short-term (issued for 13, 26 or 52 weeks), medium-term notes (issued for 2 to 7 years), and long-term bonds (up to 30 years in duration). The short-term bills (13-week and 26-week bills) are auctioned every week (usually on Mondays) in minimum amounts of $10,000 and increments of $5,000. The 52-week bills are auctioned monthly (usually on a Thursday). Unlike the long-term government bonds (see below), they are sold to investors on a discounted basis. An investor pays $10,000 in a noncompetitive bid, and immediately after the auction the government sends the buyer the interest due on the bill. At maturity, the government redeems the bill at full face value.

Risk and Rating

U.S. Treasury paper is risk-free. It will return to the investor the original face value of the purchased securities. So while Treasury paper has no credit risk, there is interest-rate risk.

Private agencies do not rate U.S. Treasury paper. Foreign buyers of American debt are an increasing influence in this market. Up to a quarter of Treasury obligations are being bought by foreign investors in recent years as U.S. deficits have reached unprecedented levels. Any buyer of government paper should be aware of foreign sentiment when considering Treasury paper. Negative foreign sentiment about the U.S. economy, the level of the U.S. dollar vis-a-vis other currencies, and the prevailing interest rates are bound to influence the prices of T-bills, notes and bonds.

Maturity and Duration

Given the breadth of Treasury obligations, you can choose exactly when you wish to redeem your funds. The business section of most daily newspapers lists the whole range of prices. Notes are not *callable*; that is, the government will not attempt to redeem them before their maturity date.

Income and Yield

Treasury bills are sold on a discounted basis. The interest is equal to the differences between the discounted price as sold at the auction and the face value. In other words, the bills are sold at a price determined by the auction. They are redeemed, however, at the full par value. The difference between what you pay for the bill and what is eventually paid back to you is the discount. The discount is the interest payment, and the yield is the discount expressed as a percentage.

Special Benefits

The interest on all Treasury paper is taxable by the federal government, but escapes taxation from city and state. Income from Treasury obligations in retirement, pension or other tax-advantaged accounts is totally tax-free until the proceeds are withdrawn.

How To Buy Treasury Bills

One of the pleasant surprises in buying T-bills is the immediate payment of interest. When you send the Treasury $10,000, it returns the interest as soon as the auction takes place. This practice raises the interest rate, since you have earned the interest payment on less than the face amount of the T-bill. Moreover, the interest payment you receive right after the auction can be reinvested to earn additional interest.

You can buy T-bills through your local broker or bank. There is a minimum charge for handling the transaction, ranging from $25 to $60. Such fees clearly cut into the yield and are more significant when you have bought a $10,000 bill than one for $100,000.

Individuals submit noncompetitive bids; the competitive ones are for the dealers and institutional participants who make the market. A noncompetitive bid guarantees the buyer the average yield and equivalent price as determined by the accepted competitive bids or tenders.

You can buy T-bills directly from one of the dozen regional Federal Reserve Banks (plus their branches). If you intend to make T-bills part of your permanent portfolio, it pays to establish an account (called Treasury Direct) with the Fed, since there is no charge for this service. The Treasury no longer issues certificates, but sends you a statement of account showing what you own. All interest is credited to your designated bank account.

Figuring Your Yield

Since there is no coupon rate and the bills are sold at a discount, you should calculate your yield to see just how competitive it is. The discount is based on the return as a percent of the face value of the bill, not the purchase price. In brief, it understates the true or actual yield. You are getting more for your funds than you anticipated. If you bought a one-year $10,000 bill selling at a 10 percent discount, you would pay $9,000 for it. Since it will be worth $10,000 at maturity, the interest on your $9,000 ($1000 ÷ $9000) is 11.11 percent. In addition, you will get interest on the $1,000 if you don't spend it.

The following is the formula for figuring your approximate bank yield from the discount:

$$\frac{\text{Face value} - \text{Purchase price}}{\text{Purchase price}} \times \frac{365\,\text{days}}{\text{Number of days to maturity}}$$

This formula gives the simple annual interest rate. For example:

$$\frac{10,000 - 9,691.60}{9,691.60} \times \frac{365}{182} = .063818\,\text{or}\,6.38\%$$

If you know the amount of the discount in dollars, you can figure the yield.

$$\text{Discount} = \frac{\text{Days to maturity}}{360} \times \text{Rate}$$

Using $100 of face value, the dollar price of a T-bill due in 150 days and trading on a 8 percent discounted basis would have the following discount:

$$150 \div 360 \times 8\% = 3.33\%$$

With a discount of $3.33 per $100 of face value, a $10,000 bill has a discount of $333 ($3.33 × 100). The price is face value less the dollar discount—$10,000 − $333 = $9,667.

If you are buying T-bills at the auction, the yield, the discount and the price are immediately published and known. There is no mystery with a new issue. You can buy

TABLE 4.1   Sample Table of U.S. Treasury Bills

Maturity Date	Bid	Asked	Bid Change	Yield
3-22-90	7.59	7.56	. . .	7.80
3-29-90	7.53	7.56	+ .03	7.81
4-05-90	7.63	7.59	+ .08	7.85

a T-bill without waiting for the auction, and for virtually any maturity. The financial press carries charts like the sample one in Table 4.1.

T-bill prices are quoted in terms of their (annual) discount rate, rather than in terms of their dollar price. For the March 29 issue in Table 4.1, the 7.53 percent indicates the discount rate derived from the bid price dealers will pay to buy from sellers, and the 7.56 percent figure indicates the discount rate resulting from the offered price at which dealers will sell T-bills to buyers. The true yield was 7.81 percent. When reading the newspaper tables, you must remember the basic rule that as yields rise prices fall.

The true bond equivalent yield uses 365 days rather than the 360 days used in Treasury bill discount quotations. You must use the bond equivalent yield to compare the yield of T-bills to savings accounts, certificates of deposit, or bonds (whether corporates, municipals or governments).

The formula for converting T-bill yields to the true bond yield is:

$$\frac{365 \times \text{Discount yield rate}}{360 - (\text{Discount yield rate} \times \text{Days to maturity})}$$

For example, if a 90-day T-bill has a 8 percent discount, what is the true bond yield?

$$\frac{365 \times .08}{360 - (.08 \times 90)} = \frac{29.2}{352.8} = 8.28\%$$

The 8 percent discount is equivalent to an 8.28 percent true bond yield for 91 days.

To save time, Table 4.2 compares the discount rate and the investment or bond equivalent yield on an annual basis.

U.S. TREASURY NOTES AND BONDS

Description

The government guarantee also applies to longer-term securities. While T-bills are purchased by many people as a safe haven to park funds temporarily, Treasury notes and bonds are long-term commitments. Treasury notes are obligations that mature between two and ten years; bonds mature between 10 and 30 years.

Risk and Rating

As with all other fixed-interest, negotiable debt instruments, Treasury notes and bonds are subject to interest rate pressures. This means that after they are issued, their price will fluctuate in relation to interest rate moves. The price goes down if interest rates go up, goes up if interest rates go down. For longer-term instruments, these price fluctuations can be quite great. Interest rate fluctuations will not affect you if you hold these securities to redemption. But they can cause loss (or gain) in principal if you are obliged to sell because of an emergency or change of plans. U.S. notes and bonds are not rated by the statistical services.

TABLE 4.2   Comparison of Discount Rate and Investment or Bond
Equivalent Yield Annually

Discount Rate Bond	Equivalent Yield
6	6.38
6.5	6.94
7	7.64
7.5	8.07
8	8.82
8.5	9.43
9	10.04
9.5	10.66
10	11.28

Maturity and Duration

A great range of maturities is available in the vast
secondary market, most of which is traded over the counter.
It is here that you can customize your portfolio and get the
exact maturities you wish. You can find issues for almost
any month or any year, from now to 30 years in the future.

If you wish to buy a new Treasury note or bond, the
general schedule for Treasury auctions is as follows:

- Quarterly financing in February, May, August and No-
  vember usually includes one three-year note, one ten-
  year note, and one 30-year bond.
- A two-year note is usually issued at the end of each
  month.
- A four-year note is usually issued at the end of March,
  June, September and December.
- A five-year note is usually issued in March, June,
  September and December.
- A seven-year note is usually issued in January, April,
  July and October.

Small investors can submit noncompetitive bids in the note and bond auctions. This assures you of a fair and reasonable price. However, the price (as determined at the auction) is not a discounted price as is the case with T-bills. Notes usually come in denominations of $5,000, $10,000, $100,000 and $1 million, and occasionally as little as $1,000. Bonds come in denominations of $1,000, $5,000, $10,000, $50,000, $100,000, and $1 million. The auction determines the coupon rate, and the instruments are sold at close to par (100).

They are sold at auction, with a minimum of $5,000 for two-year or three-year notes, but as little as a $1,000 minimum for notes and bonds with maturities of four years or more. Notes and bonds can be bought through banks and brokerage houses, though there is a nominal charge for the convenience ($25 to $60 per issue regardless of denomination). This has the effect of fractionally lowering the yield. When you purchase Treasury notes and bonds in this way, you obtain the noncompetitive average yield and equivalent price determined by the accepted competitive tenders. The competitive bids are those from broker/dealers and institutions.

Notes are not callable, that is, they are redeemed at their stated maturity. Some bond issues, however, are callable, that is they may be redeemed by the Treasury five years before their maturity dates. This enables the government to refinance high coupon bonds with lower ones to save on interest charges. If you hold or buy high coupon bonds, be aware that they may be called before you anticipated. Besides knowing the yield to maturity, in such cases it is important to know the yield to call as well.

Income and Yield

Since notes and bonds are not discounted, you pay full face value. At the auction, the Treasury determines the coupon rate to equal the competitive bidder's yield bid. As a noncompetitive bidder, you do not have to worry about missing the market, since you have agreed ahead of time to accept the average yield and price. A noncompetitive bid is allowed up to $1 million worth of any issue.

Yields on Treasury notes and bonds are *bellwether* indicators—they set the levels for all the other bond markets. They are the best guides to the true cost of risk-free capital.

Special Benefits

Treasury obligations are free of state and local taxes. The federal government does, however, collect revenue on its own bonds.

Pricing

Treasury notes and bonds have very tight markets, that is, the bid-and-offered spread is so narrow that prices are denominated in 32nds (and occasionally in 64ths) of a percentage point. Table 4.3 gives you a quick reference of the decimal equivalencies.

The financial press carries a price list that gives information for Treasury bonds and notes, for example:

Rate	Maturity	Bid	Asked	Bid Change	Yield
8/14	12-91	97.7	97.11	– .6	9.32

TABLE 4.3   Decimal Equivalencies for Treasury Notes and Bonds

1/32	.031250	17/32	.531250
2/32	.062500	18/32	.562500
3/32	.093750	19/32	.593750
4/32	.125000	20/32	.625000
5/32	.156250	21/32	.656250
6/32	.187500	22/32	.687500
7/32	.218750	23/32	.718750
8/32	.250000	24/32	.750000
9/32	.281250	25/32	.781250
10/32	.312500	26/32	.812500
11/32	.343750	27/32	.843750
12/32	.375000	28/32	.875000
13/32	.406250	29/32	.906250
14/32	.437500	30/32	.937500
15/32	.468750	31/32	.968750
16/32	.500000	32/32	1.000000

The bid price (the price at which a dealer will buy) is 97.7, or 97 7/32nds, which is equal to 97.218750 or $972.19. The asked price (the price at which a dealer will sell) is 97.11, or 97.343750, or $973.43. The bid is −.6, or −.18750 less than the day before. This issue of 8 1/4s is offering a yield to maturity of 9.32 based on the asked price. If there is a plus sign after the quotation, the issue is being quoted in 64ths—1/64 plus the price. If there are two maturity dates, the first is the possible call date, and the second is the final redemption date.

If you can buy the new issue at the auction, you will be paid semiannual interest, commencing at the issue date, plus six months. Should you buy in the secondary market, you are obliged to pay the accrued interest to the previous owner. If you sell bonds before the interest payment, you will be the recipient of the interest due. The interest is calculated on a daily basis. If you had bought the above 8 1/4s halfway through the semi-annual payment period, you would be obliged to pay 90 days of interest to the previous owner (8.25 ÷ 365 = .0226027 per day) or 90 × .0226027 = $20.34 per $1,000 bond.

Safety is never an issue with U.S. government securities, but the government does not guarantee that the money you will receive is equivalent in purchasing power to the money you invested. The record shows that the decades of the Seventies and Eighties were not reassuring on this matter. While yields on long-term government paper may be seductive, you must look for capital appreciation elsewhere—either in deep discount bonds, depressed issues or in the stock market—if your investment goal is capital appreciation.

Another alternative to capital appreciation within the bond market is to buy bonds when prices are low and yields are high, and to sell them when bonds are high and yields are low. Purchasing power and capital appreciation aside, the safety and a reasonable return on one's funds attract most investors to long-term government issues.

ZERO COUPON BONDS

Description

One of the most creative innovations in the Eighties, zero coupon bonds gained almost instant popularity when they were introduced. A zero coupon bond pays no semi-annual interest, as is customarily the case. It is not issued at par, but at a deep discount from its face value. For example, a $1,000 zero might be issued at $172 with a 9 percent incremental growth to mature in 20 years. Every year it grows in value as it matures. It finally reaches par value, $1,000, on its redemption date. The rapidity with which it appreciates is a reflection of the interest rates that prevailed at the time it was issued.

The idea of zeros was developed by two investment banking houses, Salomon Brothers and Merrill Lynch. Initially, they bought long-term Treasury bonds and deposited them with an independent custodian—a bank or trust company. Against the Treasury bonds, they issued certificates.

The zero coupon bonds are called CATS (Certificates of Accrual on Treasury Securities) by Salomon Brothers and (TIGRS) Treasury Investment Growth Receipts by Merrill Lynch. While they are not Treasury securities, they are tantamount to them.

In 1985 the Treasury, seeing a good thing, brought out its own version, called STRIPS (Separate Trading of Registered Interest and Principal of Securities). Because they are purchased at deep discounts, these instruments can triple, quadruple and even quintuple your original investment, given the miracle of compound interest.

Risk and Rating

Since these zeros are issued by the Treasury or are backed by Treasury securities, there is no credit risk. Zeros are not rated by the financial services. However, they fluctuate far more than any other fixed-interest obligation, since they provide no income stream. If you buy them with the idea of holding them to maturity, that should not matter.

Maturity and Duration

Zeros can be bought to mature in February, May, August and November for as far out as 30 years. There is an active secondary market, so you can readily sell your zeros before the maturity date if necessary.

Income and Yield

The beauty of zero coupon bonds is that they lock in a given interest rate the moment they are bought. Moreover, since you receive no interest until maturity (or until they are sold), you are spared one of the most critical problems in bond investing—what to do with the semiannual interest income as it comes due.

The flip side is that you will find it difficult to take advantage of a trend toward higher interest rates. But the disadvantage will protect you if rates go down. In short, the yield to maturity is known on the day a zero bond is purchased. You can buy a few zeros at a time—there is no such thing as a minimum quantity.

Special Benefits

Zero coupon bonds are best for retirement accounts or other tax-advantaged accounts on which no taxes are paid until money is withdrawn. If you hold zeros in an ordinary investment portfolio, the Internal Revenue Service requires owners to pay tax on the annual earned increment, even though you do not receive it. In other words, it can cost you money to own these securities in a regular account. There are zero municipal bonds (alternately called M-CATS, Municipal Receipts or compound interest bonds) which of course yield less but spare you the problem of negative cash flow. In addition, you can invest in zero corporate bonds, which are issued at deep discount. They offer a higher yield than Treasury bonds, but then they are taxable in regular accounts.

The popularity of zeros soared after the October 19, 1987, meltdown. Individual investors wanted to set targets and achieve them with a specific portion of their portfolio. Zeros were perfect for building a nest egg, a college tuition fund or a pension plan.

What Price Zeros?

Zeros are issued deeply discounted and start their lives at $50, $100 or $200 for a $1,000 face value bond, depending on issue and interest rate. Moreover, you can purchase a few at a time—there is no odd-lot penalty, though it might pay to do some comparison shopping from broker to broker. Even the dealer's spread can be eliminated by buying the issues new, since no commission is charged for original distribution of Treasury bonds. There is a broad secondary market in case you wish to sell before maturity.

The yield on zeros is often a few *basis points* (a basis point is 1/100 of 1 percent) more than comparable Treasury bonds. There is no credit risk with zeros, since they are either Treasury bonds or based on Treasury bonds. However, there is considerable interest-rate risk for investors who do not anticipate holding these bonds to maturity. Zero coupon bonds fluctuate far more than interest-bearing ones. Though the price moves up inexorably to face value, the trip can be full of potholes. A sudden surge in interest rates may depress their value.

On the other hand, a drop in interest rates can raise their price substantially. Most individual investors follow a strategy of buy and hold, but speculators and traders do take advantage of the whipsaw action of zeros in a volatile interest rate environment to trade them for capital gains. There is one rule of thumb to measure the fluctuations: If rates rise (or fall) by 1 percentage point, the value of a zero

TABLE 4.4   Sample Table of Stripped Securities

Maturity Date	Bid	Asked	Bid Change	Yield
11-04	30.60	30.23	– .4	8.10
2-05	29.17	30.20	– .4	8.11
5-05	28.31	29.15	– .4	8.11

will appreciate (or depreciate) by 1 percent for each year remaining until maturity.

The value of zeros is easy to find. Newspapers will give you daily market prices. For example, say you are interested in buying zeros for a college fund. You wish to have the funds available in 15 years. To get an idea of what 15-year zeros will cost, consult the business section of the daily paper. You will find a table of zeros (Table 4.4).

In the table, zeros are being quoted 29.17 bid, 30.2 asked, for a yield of 8.11 percent for maturity in February, 2005.

You can also use Table 4.5 to find a theoretical price, and what the zeros are worth when interest rates change.

To find the price, first locate the prevailing interest rate, 8 percent, on the top horizontal line. Then read down the vertical line, years to maturity, to find 15. At the juncture, the theoretical price is $308.

If the prevailing interest rate changes later on, you can find the theoretical market price from the table. Say, for example, that a year later in the above example, interest rates move to 10 percent. On the years to maturity, locate 14, then in the 10 percent column find the new price, $255. This is also an example of the volatility of zeros. While the price fluctuation does not alter the price at maturity, it does show that it is possible to have a major paper loss of nearly 20 percent when interest rates went up.

TABLE 4.5 Zero Values

Years to Maturity	$ Value 8%	$ Value 9%	$ Value 10%	$ Value 11%	$ Value 12%	$ Value 13%	$ Value 14%
30	$ 95	$ 71	$ 54	$ 40	$ 30	$ 23	$ 17
29	103	78	59	45	34	26	20
28	111	85	85	50	38	29	23
27	120	93	72	56	43	33	26
26	130	101	79	62	48	38	30
25	141	111	87	69	54	43	34
24	152	121	96	77	61	49	39
23	165	132	106	85	69	55	45
22	178	144	117	95	77	63	51
21	193	157	129	106	87	71	58
20	208	172	142	117	97	81	67
19	225	188	157	131	109	91	76
18	244	205	173	146	123	104	88
17	264	224	190	162	138	118	100
16	285	245	210	180	155	133	115
15	308	267	231	201	174	151	131
14	333	292	255	223	196	171	150
13	361	318	281	249	220	195	172
12	390	348	310	277	247	221	197
11	422	380	342	308	278	250	226
10	456	415	377	343	312	284	258
9	494	453	416	381	350	322	296
8	534	494	458	425	394	365	339
7	577	540	505	473	442	414	388
6	625	590	557	526	597	470	444
5	676	644	614	585	558	533	508
4	731	703	677	652	627	604	582
3	790	768	746	725	705	685	666
2	855	839	823	807	792	777	763
1	925	916	907	899	890	882	873
0	1,000	1,000	1,000	1,000	1,000	1,000	1,000

Real prices are, of course, determined by supply and demand, plus the normal dealer spread. Therefore, the theoretical value is meant only as a guide.

Y · O · U · R   M · O · V · E

- Reserve some portion of your overall portfolio for these forms of government guaranteed debt. The more anxious you are about risking your money, the more you should consider Treasury obligations. Whether your portfolio should have 10 or 50 percent depends on your anxiety quotient. In rough economic weather, you may wisely decide to be 100 percent in Treasuries.
- Since no one is smart enough to know the top in the interest rate cycle, buy your Treasury notes and bonds over a period of time for the best average price and yield.
- Stagger maturities, especially in the case of zero coupon bonds, so that the tax bill does not become too oppressive in one year.
- Any time long-term bond yields have exceeded 10 percent or more, it presents a "window of opportunity" for astute investors.
- Investors who believe that a portion of their portfolio should be in Treasuries can increase their yields (and lower their commission costs) by opening a Treasury Direct account with their local Federal Reserve Bank.
- Remember that Treasury bills, notes and bonds are free of state and local taxation—another real boost to your after-tax income.

S · H · O · R · T · C · U · T

U.S. Government Bond Funds

- Benham Treasury Note Fund
- Fidelity Government Securities Fund

- Lord Abbett U.S. Government Securities
- Putnam U.S. Government Guaranteed Securities
- Value Line U.S. Government Securities
- Van Kampen Merritt U.S. Government

• 5 •

Federal Agency Securities: Higher Government Interest Rates

ARE THEY DIFFERENT
FROM TREASURIES?

One of the least known corners of the fixed-income field, debt obligations of the federal government's agencies offer some of the highest yields of all government paper. Agency securities do not always have the explicit guarantee of the U.S. Treasury, but the federal government has never allowed any of its agency debt to default—nor is it likely to.

Although it may be assumed that agency securities are as safe as Treasury securities, you should not assume that there is no difference between these two types of securities. Some of the differences are as follows:

- Agency securities are underwritten by investment banks, and so cannot be purchased directly from issuing agencies.
- Individual investors cannot buy all agency securities, since some are issued only in large denominations.
- The market in agency debt is less active, which in turn means that the spread between selling price and asking price is likely to be wider than for comparable Treasury securities. Though the yields may be higher in agency

debt, a small investor may have to pay more to buy or sell for less.

However, the major appeal of agency securities is the higher return than can be obtained from Treasury securities. Generally speaking, there is an advantage of 25 to 75 *basis points*, though on occasion it exceeds 100 basis points.

In brief, the agencies offer a slightly higher yield, both to attract investors and to overcome the perception of slightly more credit risk compared to Treasuries.

Almost two dozen agencies and government-sponsored corporations issue negotiable notes and *debentures* (debt securities without any collateral backing). The financial pages in newspapers list most actively traded agencies:

- Federal National Mortgage Association (FNMA or Fannie Mae)
- Federal Home Loan Banks
- Government National Mortgage Association (GNMA or Ginnie Mae)
- Student Loan Marketing
- Federal Land Banks
- World Bank
- Inter-American Development Bank

Domestic agency securities largely fall into two groups, those that help farming and agriculture, and those that assist in home mortgages.

Description

The market for agency securities is smaller than for the Treasury market. Prices are more easily affected by public perceptions than Treasury securities. If an agency has problems (such as the Farm Credit System does with failing farms or the Federal Home Loan Bank does with the troubled savings and loan associations), their prices will fall and yields will rise.

These bonds are denominated in $1,000 units, but frequently the minimum purchase is set at $25,000. Agency securities are not auctioned: they are underwritten by syndicates of investment bankers who in turn sell them to investors. The syndicate dealers make a secondary market for the issues they underwrite.

Both bearer and book entry issues are available.

Risk and Rating

Though the Treasury does not issue them, these securities are either government-guaranteed or government-sponsored. Thus while most of them do not have explicit government backing that Treasury securities have, the federal government has never failed to assist these agencies when they have gotten into difficulties. Most observers consider them risk-free investments, though they do fluctuate in price. The risk is slightly greater than with Treasury securities, but history has yet to show investors sustaining a loss—nor is it likely.

Securities of the agencies are not rated by the statistical services, nor are they registered with the Securities and Exchange Commission.

Maturity and Duration

Federal agency securities have maturity dates that range up to 30 years. Fifteen-year maturities are most common, and the agencies often issue short-term notes that mature in two or five years. As a rule, there are no early call provisions, so an investor can be assured of a yield to maturity. Shorter-term securities can be found in Federal Land Bank bonds and the farm credit agencies. Longer-term paper is available in Government National Mortgage Association and Federal National Mortgage Association bonds.

Income and Yield

If you are a small investor, it is hard to be active in this market, since securities are often available only in minimum denominations of $5,000 or $10,000, and in some cases $25,000. Interest is paid semiannually. The return on agency securities tracks the Treasury yield curve.

Special Benefits

Income from agency securities are taxable at the federal level, but are usually free of state and local taxation. If these securities are bought in a tax-exempt account, the interest is not taxed until it is withdrawn.

Agricultural Debt

The farm credit agencies designed to promote farming and agriculture are the Banks for Cooperatives, the Federal Intermediate Credit Banks, and the Federal Land Banks. They all operate under the auspices of the Farm Credit Administration—an independent agency of the U.S. government that is responsible for the cooperative farm credit system. Each of the three agencies issues their own securities to investors and then lends the proceeds to the agricultural sector.

The Bank for Cooperatives (Co-ops) was formed during the Great Depression to supply credit to farmers' cooperative organizations. The agency is now a private corporation owned by the cooperative organizations. There is a bank in each of the nation's 12 farm credit districts, plus a central bank in Washington. The agency issues debentures in $5,000 and $10,000 units for small investors, plus increments of $1,000. They are not callable before their maturity dates. While free of state and local taxes, they are subject to federal income tax.

The Federal Intermediate Credit Banks (FICBs) are a dozen privately owned banks that lend capital to lending institutions that serve the farming sector. They obtain their funds from the regular sale of debentures in $5,000 and $10,000. They too are not callable, but they are exempt from city and state taxes, though subject to federal taxation.

The third agricultural institution is the 12 Federal Land Banks (FLBs). They borrow from the investing public by issuing Consolidated Federal Farm Loan bonds. They then use the proceeds for long-term real estate loans. These bond issues are not callable and are available in bearer or book-entry form, depending on the length of maturities. Small denominations are available, starting with $1,000, plus $5,000 and $10,000 units. This issue has the lowest minimum purchase requirement—$1,000—of any government agency. They too are not guaranteed by the Treasury and are exempt from city and state taxes.

All these issuing agencies have a range of older maturities in the marketplace. In recent years, they have taken to issuing their bonds under the aegis of the Federal Farm Credit system, which is regulated by the Farm Credit Administration. When the system needs funds, it issues a wide range of debt instruments, from discounted notes (similar to Treasury bills) to longer-term bonds, from six months to 15 years. Although they are exempt from local taxes, they are not callable and are subject to federal taxation.

Home Mortgage Securities

The second major group of agency issues falls into the category of mortgage bonds. The Federal Home Loan Bank (FHLB) system was established in 1932 to regulate the thrift industry, that collection of savings and loan associations, savings banks and insurance companies that provide credit for home mortgages.

Though the FHLB is owned by the thrift institutions, it is federally chartered and can be considered an agency of the U.S. government. The continuing injection of funds into the deeply troubled savings and loan industry shows that Congress is indeed backing the securities of the industry.

To generate funds for its banks to lend to homeowners (in addition to the funds they take in as deposits), the FHLB must borrow in the open market. It issues notes and consolidated bonds in denominations of $10,000 and up (in $5,000 increments). They are not callable, and they are subject to federal taxation, though not state and local taxes.

The oldest mortgage association is the Federal National Mortgage Association (FNMA), informally known as Fannie Mae. It is a government-sponsored corporation wholly owned by private stockholders, and the shares are traded on the New York Stock Exchange. Originally it was established to provide liquidity for government-guaranteed or government-insured mortgages of the Veterans Administration or the Federal Housing Administration. Presently, it buys mortgages when money is tight and sells mortgages when money is abundant.

To finance its operations, Fannie Mae issues short-term notes and bonds. It also issues securities backed by pools of mortgages guaranteed by another government agency, the Government National Mortgage Association (GNMA), or Ginnie Mae. The debentures are available in $10,000 and $25,000 units (in addition to larger denominations), with a minimum of $10,000 for the debentures, but a minimum of $50,000 for the short-term notes. The yields are perhaps slightly higher than comparable agency paper, since they are not exempt from federal, state or local taxation.

Pricing Agency Issues

The more popular issues are quoted in the financial section of the newspaper are for trades of $1 million or more. If you are looking for $10,000 or $25,000 of these bonds, you will have to pay a bit more—a factor which lowers the yield. Try to buy such issues when they are new so that you can avoid any commission or any concession in price.

Under "Government and Agency Issues" in the newspaper, you will find a long list of FNMA securities, among other agency issues. For example:

Rate	Maturity	Bid	Asked	Yield
11.75	12-95	105-23	106-01	9.25

The 11.75 percent FNMA issue maturing in December 1995 is being bid on by dealers (who will buy from the public) at 105 23/32 ($1057.18750 per $1,000 bond). They are asking (or offering to sell these bonds to the public) at 106 1/32 (or $1060.31250 per $1,000 bond). This issue is selling at a premium, since the prevailing interest rates are somewhat lower than the 11.75 coupon attached to the issue. Finally, the yield to maturity is 9.25 percent.

Your broker should be aware of upcoming issues. (For additional information about selecting a broker see *The Basics of Stocks*, Chapter 9. Some discount brokers either have no inventory of agency paper or do not execute trades in government securities.) You may also see new issues advertised in the financial pages by the underwriting syndicate that is issuing the securities a few days before the offering.

With an indication of interest, your broker may be able to obtain some bonds, especially if the brokerage firm was part of the underwriting syndicate. Round lots in the agency world are $100,000, but you may be able to buy fewer bonds at the initial offering. Desirable issues are snapped up by institutions, but there may be some tag ends for individuals. Moreover, syndicates maintain an after-market, and it is possible to purchase issues after they have been issued. The most active markets and the ones with the smallest spreads are the most recent issues.

MORTGAGE-BACKED SECURITIES

Description

Bonds are not the only securities that federal agencies issue. In recent years, mortgage-backed securities have become a major source of funds for some agencies. These mortgage-backed bonds are called *pass-through certificates,* since they pass on to their holders interest and principal on a regular and timely basis.

To encourage home ownership, the federal government established a series of mortgage associations to buy mortgages from the local banks and savings and loan associations that had originated them. The three chief issuers of these certificates are: Government National Mortgage Association (GNMA or Ginnie Mae); Federal National Mortgage Association (FNMA or Fannie Mae); Federal Home Loan Mortgage Corporation (FHLMC or Freddie Mac).

Ginnie Mae guarantees timely payments of principal and interest, and its issues are backed by the full faith and credit pledge of the Treasury. The securities of Fannie Mae and Freddie Mac also guarantee timely payments of principal and interest. However, they are not directly guaranteed by the government, though no one doubts that the government would assist them if they were in trouble. This anomaly causes slightly higher yields for Fannie Mae and Freddie Mac certificates than for those of Ginnie Mae. If you want the higher yield, perhaps 25 basis points, buy FNMA or FHLMC securities, but if you want total safety, buy GNMA certificates.

By supplying funds to lending organizations, the government was increasing the availability of mortgage money, especially in the late Seventies and early Eighties, when interest rates were high and mortgage money was scarce. Mortgages are ideal credit instruments, since homeowners are likely to give their mortgage payments first priority when writing out the month's checks. This tends to ensure that the mortgage pools will have a steady cash flow from the mortgage payments, both as to principal and interest.

These government mortgage agencies create pools of these home mortgages and sell participation certificates in these pools of mortgages to private investors. These securities then receive monthly proceeds from the agency as mortgage payments are passed through and relatively small service charges are deducted. Each mortgage pool has its own special characteristics in terms of size, kind and the rates available.

While the pools are established for 20 or 30 years to coincide with the terms of the underlying mortgages, in practice they are paid off on an average of 12 years. The early retirement can be traced to early prepayment by some mortgage holders as they sell their current home to buy another one, or as they refinance their mortgage at more advantageous rates. The repossession of some homes when mortgage payments are in default will also lead to early retirement.

Risk and Rating

In light of these variations, the interest rates on such certificates cannot be predicted with any certainty. Though the interest rates are not guaranteed, the repayment of the principal is guaranteed by the federal agencies that issue the certificates, sometimes with or without the blessings of the federal government or the Federal Reserve System. So while some agency paper is not the direct obligation of the U.S. government, no one doubts that the government would bail out an agency if it were in temporary distress.

The risk in these agency certificates exists in both the rate of return and their sensitivity to interest-rate fluctuations in general. There are really two levels of risk. First, interest payments on the mortgages will change as a result of some of the mortgages being refinanced. Second, change in the prevailing interest rates affects the price of the obligations.

Your risk is increased by buying the highest-yielding certificates, since those are the very ones most subject to refinancing. Investors who are trying to preserve their capital should *not* reach for the highest yielding certificates, however tempting that may be. Homeowners are reluctant to pay 13 percent when they can obtain new mortgages for 10 percent.

Agency certificates are not graded by the financial rating services, since their likelihood of default is nil.

Maturity and Duration

The average life of these mortgage certificates—12 years—is dependent on the speed or the assumed prepayment rate: the faster the speed, the shorter the life and vice versa.

Income and Yield

Pass-through securities of the mortgage associations are initially sold for $25,000, with $5,000 increments. Small investors can buy *paid-down certificates*—those that have only a half or a third of a life-expectancy left.

Each mortgage pool has its own coupon rate, contingent on when it was issued. As a rule, agency certificates have paid higher rates than comparable Treasuries by a full 1 percent (100 basis points) or more. In fact, a study by one investment bank noted that during one recent five-year period, Government National Mortgage Association yields averaged about 140 basis points above those on comparable U.S. Treasury issues.

The monthly return makes them an ideal vehicle if you need continuous income. But one note of warning: The monthly payment includes both mortgage principal and interest. If you spend the principal, you will reduce your capital. Your brokerage house, if so instructed, will hold or reinvest the principal and return only the interest to you.

Special Benefits

These certificates are fully taxable at all levels of taxation. If they are placed in a tax-free account, such as one for retirement purposes, the interest income will not be taxable until the proceeds are withdrawn.

Y • O • U • R   M • O • V • E

- You should stick with issues of the major agencies. These are the ones listed in the financial press. You can buy exotic issues, but that is best left to professional investors.

- Try to buy new issues. The market for agency securities is dominated by institutional investors. If you have trouble buying small amounts ($5,000–$50,000), consider opening an account with a broker who specializes in this market. Also consider one of the mutual funds dedicated to Treasury and agency securities.

- An investor can trade agency securities, but most small investors hold them to maturity. Since you buy agency securities for safety and income, do not try to outguess the market on interest rate fluctuations. The monthly payment of mortgage-backed certificates, such as Ginnie Maes, does make them less volatile than the bonds of the various agencies which pay interest only twice a year.

- In mortgage backed pass-through securities, do not reach for the highest coupon issue, especially if it is selling at a premium. A high-interest environment virtually ensures that mortgagors will pay off or refinance their mortgages when rates markedly decrease. The pool will then be faced with prepayments which an investor will have to reinvest at lower rates. Furthermore, the price of the pass-through issue will drop, eliminating the premium, which either constitutes a capital loss or a lower yield to maturity.

- Finally, remember that the monthly payments from Ginnie Mae, Freddie Mac, or Fannie Mae pass-through issues are a combination of interest and principal. Unless you request that principal be held to be reinvested in a money market account or some other instrument, you may end up spending your capital unwittingly.

S • H • O • R • T • C • U • T

U.S. Federal Agency Funds

- FPA New Income
- Lexington GNMA Income
- Merrill Lynch Federal Securities
- Princor Government Securities Income
- SLH Income-Mortgage Securities
- Smith Barney Monthly Government

• 6 •

Municipal Bonds:
Tax-Free Investing

THE WORLD OF MUNIS

Individual investors own more municipal bonds than any other type of investment. Municipal bonds represent the debt of tens of thousands of issuing units: cities, states, agencies, authorities, municipal utilities, ports, harbors, airports and so on. They have a dual purpose, which accounts for their success: They provide cheap funds for necessary public works (like sewage plants, roads and bridges) while providing investors with tax-free income.

They fall into two categories: *general obligation bonds* (such as California State 9.5% of 10/01/99), which are funded by the taxing power of the issuers; and *revenue bonds*, (such as New Jersey Turnpike Authority 10.375% of 01/01/03) which derive their income from fees, tolls and other user assessments.

Municipal bonds are sold at face value with a fixed coupon rate in minimum denominations of $5,000. (There are some baby bonds of $1,000.) Interest is usually paid semiannually. Bonds issued after July 1983 must be in registered form, but there are many earlier issues that are in bearer form (with coupons attached).

Risk and Rating

Although a few issuers of municipal bonds have declared bankruptcy in the past, municipal bonds have very little credit risk. General obligation bonds are especially secure, since they are backed by the taxing ability of the issuer. The debt will be repaid from the collection of property and land taxes, income taxes or sales taxes, as appropriate. Revenue bonds rely on fees, tolls and other charges.

Financial rating services do pass on the creditworthiness of municipal bonds. For example, one rating agency uses ten ranks to grade municipal bonds. Only the top four are considered to be of investment quality. Bonds rated below BBB are considered speculative, that is, there is some doubt as to whether the issuer will repay the borrowed funds.

The risk inherent in some issues can be reduced by municipal bond insurance, which now comes with about a quarter of all new issues. This insurance guarantees to pay off the bondholders in case of default. The premium charge for the insurance lowers the yield slightly.

Maturity and Duration

Municipal bonds have fixed maturity dates, some up to 40 years out. Some municipals are retired in serial fashion; that is, a part of the debt is retired annually over the life of the issue. Consider investing in *serial bonds* if you are looking for a continuing stream of money to fund a college education or your retirement years.

Other municipals are all redeemed on the date the bond issue matures—these are called *term bonds*. And some bonds have a sinking fund to pay off the bonds at maturity: These bonds are often selected by lottery before maturity.

There is no way of knowing when your bonds will be called.

To protect yourself from an early call, look for bonds with call protection. If the bonds have an "early call" provision, the issuer is permitted to retire the issue before the fixed maturity date. The issuer will call the bonds early if it is possible to substitute high-coupon bonds with lower-coupon bonds. Without call protection, your high coupon bonds may be called away from you. You will not only suffer a loss of the higher rates, you will also be obliged to find a new investment in a period of lower interest rates.

Another form of protection is *put bonds*. These bonds have a provision that allows the bondholder to return to the issuer the bond at par value whenever seems appropriate or in accordance with a schedule. The proceeds can then be invested in higher yielding instruments.

Income and Yield

If you buy a new issue, the coupon rate determines the yield. You will receive that fixed rate for the life of the bond. If you buy a bond in the secondary market, be aware of two distinct yields: the coupon yield and the yield to maturity.

If the bonds are bought at par and are expected to be held to maturity, then the coupon is the yield to maturity. If the bonds are bought at a premium, then the yield to maturity is going to be less. Conversely, if the bonds are bought at a discount, then the yield to maturity will be more.

If the price is at a discount, brokers will quote yield to maturity. There is not likely to be a call while current interest rates are higher than the coupon rate.

If the price is at a premium, the yield to call rate is preferred since they may well be called to reduce interest costs to the issuer.

Prices on municipal bonds are usually quoted as yields or the basis price. (For further information on yields, see Chapter 2.)

Special Benefits

The Tax Reform Act of 1986 established four classes of municipal bonds with varying tax-exempt characteristics. You must be familiar with these types if you are to obtain the maximum tax benefits.

- Bonds issued before August 7, 1986, remain tax-free.
- Newer bonds issued for "public purposes" are also tax-free.
- Bonds issued for nongovernmental purposes are considered as *preference items* in calculating alternative minimum taxes.
- Fully taxable municipals may be exempt from local taxes, but are not exempt from federal taxation.

The interest on municipal bonds is tax-free, but any capital gain you realize from trading bonds is fully taxable.

Tax-Free Investing

The rewards from tax-free investing are so obvious that they need no promotion. In a world where taxes travel in only one direction—up—tax-advantaged investing is a necessity if you wish to increase your after-tax income.

Municipal bonds are based on the taxing authorities and revenue-raising abilities of towns, cities and states, and a whole host of districts, authorities and institutions created for special purposes. This ability to levy taxes and raise fees makes them almost as safe as Treasury paper. Thus, safety of your principal is generally ensured from their power to tax. Also ensured is the fixed income derived from the semiannual interest payments.

The most desirable feature of municipal bonds is their tax exempt nature. States and municipalities may not tax federal facilities or obligations, and conversely bonds of states and municipalities are free of federal taxation. Holders of municipal bonds are exempt from federal taxation and from local taxation if the obligations are issued within the state of residence. This exemption has long historic precedent, and it is not likely to be lost under new revenue reform acts.

The Tax Reform Act of 1986 eliminated many deductions and subjected virtually all income to taxation. Though it meant to simplify taxation, it complicated the world of tax-free income and municipal bonds.

You should be familiar with the basic tax rates set by the new tax code in order to determine whether you can profit from municipal bonds. (See Table 6.1.)

WHAT DOES TAX EXEMPTION MEAN TO YOU?

Quite simply, tax exemption allows you to increase and hold more of your investment income. Suppose you have $10,000 invested in 6 percent tax-exempt bonds—you will receive $600 a year in tax-free income.

If you have $10,000 invested at 6 percent in taxable bonds, you will receive $600 a year of taxable interest. In the 15 percent tax bracket, you will have $510 in after-tax income, and in the 28 percent bracket you will have only

TABLE 6.1 Tax Rate Schedules

If Your Income Is Over	But Not Over	Tax Rate
For single taxpayers:		
$ 0	$20,350	15%
$20,350	$49,300	28%
$49,300	no limit	31%
For married couples filing jointly:		
$ 0	$34,000	15%
$34,000	$82,150	28%
$82,150	no limit	31%

$432. The higher your tax bracket, the more disadvantageous are taxable bonds compared to tax-exempt bonds.

Look at it the other way. How much would you have to earn in a *taxable* investment to equal the earnings of a tax-free investment? To determine the equivalent coupon rate to match a tax-free municipal, use the following formula:

$$\frac{\text{Tax-free coupon rate}}{100\% - \text{Tax bracket}}$$

The equivalent of a tax-free 7 percent municipal bond for someone in the 28 percent bracket is:

$$\frac{7\%}{100\% - 28\%} = 9.72\%$$

Table 6.2 compares tax-free yields with taxable yields.

Furthermore, the Tax Reform Act of 1986 adjusted the minimum tax, known as the *alternative minimum tax*. This is a flat tax of 21 percent that is applied to all of your earnings, especially income that is not taxed for the purposes of calculating your personal income tax.

TABLE 6.2   Comparison of Tax-Free Yields to Taxable Yields

	Equivalent Taxable Yields		
Tax-Free Yield	*15%*	*28%*	*31%*
4.00	4.71	5.56	5.80
5.00	5.88	6.94	7.25
6.00	7.65	8.33	8.70
7.00	8.24	9.72	10.14
8.00	9.41	11.11	11.59
9.00	10.59	12.50	13.04
10.00	11.76	13.89	14.49
11.00	12.94	15.28	15.94
12.00	14.12	16.67	17.39

The alternative minimum tax applies when it exceeds your regular income tax—therefore, both calculations have to be made. The regulations are complicated, but in essence all *preference items* (such as passive losses from tax shelters and investments, and income on private activity bonds or exempt-interest dividends) are considered preference items. Therefore, it is important to be aware of which of the four categories of municipal bonds you are acquiring.

The advantage of tax-free income rests on three factors:

1. The coupon rate for municipals
2. The prevailing interest rate for taxable securities of equal or better credit such as government bonds
3. The individual (or couple's joint) tax bracket

These variables are always in a state of flux, but with some patience you can ascertain the best entry point to lock in excellent long-term, tax-free yields.

The coupon rate for municipal bonds has ranged widely over the years—from 1.29 percent in 1946 to 13.44 percent in 1982. In 1991, the Bond Buyer Municipal Bond Index was yielding 6.90 percent, whereas 30-year Treasury bonds were yielding 7.95 percent and Barron's Best Grade corporates were yielding 8.56 percent.

At times, the difference between municipals and Treasury yields narrows until there is barely 1 percent (100 basis points) differential. When the spread is that close, it is an optimum time to buy municipal bonds. Ordinarily, the difference in the respective yields is a full 2 to 3 percentage points.

ALL MUNIS ARE NOT EQUAL!

Since tax exemption is a primary reason for buying municipal bonds, it is important to buy only the municipals that are totally tax-exempt. The Tax Reform Act of 1986 divided municipal bonds into four categories. The first category is all bonds issued before August 15, 1986. These bonds are perpetually tax-exempt.

The second category is *general obligation public purpose bonds,* which are issued by state and local governments for essential governmental functions—schools, highways, etc. These are all tax-exempt under the new tax law, even when issued after August 15, 1986.

The third category is *private activity bonds* issued by state and local authorities for the construction of such facilities as shopping malls and convention centers. Since the federal government views these facilities as nonessential, the bond issues that support them are subject to federal taxation but are exempt from state and local levies.

The fourth category is nongovernmental-purpose bonds, which support such needs as housing, dormitories or student loans. States are limited under the new tax code to a fixed dollar cap that they may spend on such facilities. For the investor, nongovernmental purpose bonds fall into a shadowy area: They are deemed to be preference items and subject to the alternative minimum tax. As a rule, the yields are slightly higher to compensate for their potential taxability.

Municipal bonds are either *general obligation* or *revenue bonds*. Some observers think general obligation bonds are more creditworthy, since they are backed by a pledge of unlimited taxation on all taxable property within the jurisdiction. Other observers find the history of revenue bonds comforting since the revenues, fees and charges generated by airports, sewers, industrial development parks and other key facilities have proven to be an excellent funding source.

General obligation bonds are analyzed and evaluated on the basis of the resources available for taxation. Revenue bonds, on the other hand, are judged on the specific project's earnings capabilities. In reality, there is no easy way for an investor to judge the creditworthiness of a municipal bond issue, regardless of its funding source. You must rely on common sense and the rating services.

Nevertheless, some bonds are better fortified than others if they have extra features that enhance their security, safety and investment-worthiness. Here is a brief survey of some of these valuable features:

- *Double-barreled bonds* have not one but two pledges or sources of payments. Besides the taxing power of the municipality, they are backed by a special tax or assessment.
- *Limited and special tax bonds* are funded by a specific charge or tax on property or commodities.
- *Housing bonds* are based on residential mortgages that are sometimes additionally supported by the VA, FHA, or other federal housing subsidies.
- *Insured bonds* are backed by syndicates of private insurance companies, such as the Municipal Bond Investors Assurance Corporation (MBIA) and American

Municipal Bond Assurance Corporation (AMBAC). When so backed, insured bonds are given the highest ratings by the rating agencies.

- *Put bonds* give the investor an option to return the bond to the issuer. If it is a *mandatory put*, the bondholder has no option and must tender the bond on the "put date." An *optional put* gives the bondholder a variable coupon rate and a variable maturity.

- *Refunded bonds* are secured by funds placed in escrow, sometimes Treasury securities that provide sufficient monies for paying off bondholders.

You should also look at the bond issue's rating. There are over 100,000 political subdivisions in the U.S., many of which issue municipal bonds. Check their credit ratings, since in the history of municipal bonds quality has ranged far and wide. Below is an interpretation of how rating agencies such as Standard & Poor's might rate municipal debt:

Investment Grade Ratings

AAA   Capacity to pay interest and repay principal is extremely strong.

AA   Strong capacity to pay interest and repay principal, differs from the highest rated issues only in small degree.

A   Strong capacity to pay interest and repay principal although it is somewhat more susceptible to the adverse effects of changes in circumstances and economic conditions than higher rated debt.

BBB Adequate capacity to pay interest and repay principal. Normally exhibits adequate protection, but adverse economic conditions or changing circumstances are more likely to lead to a weakened capacity to pay interest and repay principal for debt in this category than in higher rated categories.

Speculative Grade Ratings

BB Less near-term vulnerability to default than other speculative issues. However, it faces major ongoing uncertainties to adverse business, financial or economic conditions, which could lead to inadequate capacity to meet timely interest and principal repayments.

B A greater vulnerability to default, but currently has the capacity to meet interest payments and principal repayments. Adverse conditions will likely impair capacity or willingness to pay interest and repay principal.

CCC Currently identifiable vulnerability to default, and is dependent on favorable conditions to meet timely payment of interest and repayment of principal.

CC Typically applied to debt subordinated to senior debt, which is assigned an actual or implied "CCC" debt rating.

C   Typically applied to debt subordinated to senior debt, which is assigned an actual or implied "CCC-" debt rating.

D   In payment default.

Plus (+) or minus (−) signs show relative standings within the major rating categories.

BUYING MUNICIPALS

Once you are aware of the four categories of tax-exempt bonds, the special benefits to be derived from some municipals, and the value of the ratings, you are ready to acquire tax-free obligations.

New issues are advertised in the financial press. Depending on the size of the underwriting and its availability, a small investor may be able to purchase some odd lots, blocks of $5,000, $10,000 or $25,000 principal amount. (A round lot in municipal bonds is considered to be $100,000.) The face value (or par value) is usually $5,000 for municipals (though some $1,000 denominations exist). If you plan to hold municipals for long periods or to maturity, the coupon rate (which is identical to the yield to maturity in new issues) is of paramount importance. It is stated in the advertising and prospectus for the new bonds.

All new bonds issues since 1983 are registered, that is, the owner is registered with the issuer or its agent for principal and interest. Some bearer bonds exist in the secondary market, but there is a concerted program to reduce their number. Bearer bonds have negotiable coupons, which can be used by those inclined to evade taxes by failing to report the income on their tax forms.

Ask your broker about the brokerage house's inventory to see if there is anything to fulfill your requirements. Or you can look in the financial press: The listings will be meager compared to what is generally available. There are probably 50,000 municipal issues in the secondary market, so there is no lack of choice. However, only a few of the more popular issues are listed in the newspapers.

If you are interested in municipal bonds, you might want to consult a number of publications as well as some specialized newsletters. The *Bond Buyer* is recognized as the industry's trade publication and it announces all upcoming underwritings. Standard & Poor's issues the *Bond Guide,* a monthly quick reference to corporate, convertible and municipal securities. It also issues the encyclopedic *Municipal Bond Book* on a monthly basis, *The Blue List* (a daily price sheet for bond traders), and the authoritative *CreditWeek* which covers the whole field of fixed-income obligations. Copies of these and other reference works are available on a subscription basis or in business libraries.

Municipal bonds are mostly quoted on a *yield-to-maturity basis* in the secondary market—it is called the basis price. In other words, they are *not* quoted on a percentage of par or dollar price basis as is common with government or corporate paper.

One of the major reasons for this practice is that large municipal issues are composed of *serial bonds,* sets of bonds that mature at different times and have different coupons. This is also one of the reasons why most municipal bonds are not quoted in the press—the mechanics would be exhaustive and overly complicated. Some prices, however, are indeed represented, but those are for *term bonds* whose quotations are in dollars, hence the nickname "dollar bonds." These dollar bonds are usually revenue bonds.

Therefore, if you ask for a price quotation, you will be quoted a yield to maturity, which for the fixed income investor is the most important figure. Thus a 5.5 percent coupon Metropolitan Transit Authority of New York maturing on July 12, 2014, may be quoted as 7.5 percent bid, 7.25 percent asked. For a current price, you (or your broker or commercial bank) will have to consult the Basis Book, a compilation of tables that gives dollar prices when yields are known. (The Yield Book does the opposite, giving the yield when the dollar price is known.)

Computers and handheld business calculators are also used to find the price, especially the desktop Monroe Trader. In this case, the Basis Book will show a bid price, say 98.25 ($982.50) per $1,000 bond. The offered price might be 99.25 ($992.50). The dealer's spread is 1 point, or $10.

Municipal bonds selling at a discount are not likely to be called, so yield to maturity is quoted. If the bonds trade at a premium, the possibility of a call exists, since the issuer is paying a coupon rate that is higher than prevailing interest rates. Therefore, premium bonds are quoted on a yield-to-call basis.

It is wise to stay with actively quoted issues, since the spread between bid and asked prices is small—1/2 ($5) to 1 ($10) point. Inactive or exotic issues can have spreads of 3 ($30) or 4 ($40) points, which certainly lowers the yield.

WHAT ABOUT INTEREST?

When you buy bonds in the secondary market, you are obliged to pay the previous owner the interest that has accumulated since the last payment. All quotations, therefore, are on a yield basis, plus accrued interest.

Municipal bonds pay interest twice a year. If you had purchased $10,000 of 6 percent bonds for delivery on August 10th and the last coupon payment was made on

April 1, you would owe the seller 4 months and 9 days' worth of interest—approximately $215 ($600 ÷ 360 = 1.66 per day, times 129 days). If the bonds were at par, your total payment to the seller would be $10,215. As the buyer, you would receive $300 from the issuer or fiscal agent on October 1, a net tax-exempt earning of $85 ($300 − $215) for the one month and 21 days you actually owned the bonds.

Not all municipal bonds pay interest. Along with the growth of Treasury zeros, the municipal bond industry has developed its own variation. In Treasury zeros, the interest is the annualized incremental value of the bonds. Unless the Treasury zeros are in a tax-deferred account (IRA, Keogh, 401(k), et al.), the Internal Revenue Service views that appreciation as taxable income. In municipal zeros, the appreciation is treated as interest income (even though you do not actually receive it) and hence is tax-exempt from federal as well as state and local taxes.

A further variation on this theme are municipals called *tax-deferred interest securities* (TDIS) or *convertible zeros,* which look like zeros for 7 to 12 years. Initially, they are sold at a deep discount from face value. At the point when they reach face value, they start to pay interest at the original offering yield on a semiannual basis until their redemption date. In other words, in the second stage of life, they act as traditional municipal bonds, and the interest payments are tax-free.

For example, you can buy five convertible zeros with a 10 percent interest rate for $1,885. In ten years, they will be worth $5,000 and will then automatically convert to a regular municipal that will pay 10 percent (semiannually) for 20 years. In 30 years, your funds will have increased about seven times, plus whatever additional interest on the interest you might earn.

Another twist on municipal zeros are called *compound-interest bonds* or *municipal multipliers.* They are, however, issued at face value and actually pay interest, though the interest is undistributed and reinvested at the original yield to maturity. Unlike Treasury strips, municipal zeros may be called in 15 years. This obviously alters the yield to maturity. There may be a premium if the zero municipals are indeed called.

SWAPPING: GAINS AND LOSSES

Municipal bonds are affected by interest rate fluctuations, as is the case with all negotiable, fixed-income investments. The cardinal rule is that as interest rates go up, principal falls, and vice versa. In the course of holding your municipal bonds, there will be years when they are selling at a premium over your purchase price, and years when they are at a discount, below your acquisition price. Many investors simply hold municipal bonds for their income—little concerned with the rise and fall of prices.

However, some investors use fluctuations to raise the current yield or the yield to maturity, or to reduce their tax liabilities. The effort to raise yields may be caused by a change in the investor's objectives: Perhaps less income is needed at present, but more will be needed in the future. You might then sell your high-yielding coupon bonds and buy deeply discounted bonds. A swap for yield must be as carefully analyzed as a new commitment—the trends in interest rates, ratings, and yields must all be considered. For small investors with a few bonds, the benefits may be outweighed by the transaction costs.

Tax swaps are advantageous, since there is great similarity in bonds—they are virtually interchangeable. Bonds of different issuers can be substituted for each other, provided the coupon rate, the rating and the maturity are all roughly comparable. Unlike common stock, the replacement of one issue with another of equal characteristics does not really change the complexion of your holdings.

However, this exchangeability can help you take advantage of the tax laws. The Internal Revenue Service allows a capital loss to reduce ordinary income by $3,000 per year. Thus, a decline in bond prices below their purchase price and subsequent sale can be used to establish the loss. You cannot buy back the same exact issue (that is considered a *wash sale* if done within 30 days, and is disallowed), but buying any other issue with similar characteristics leaves your position virtually unchanged.

In brief, a bond swap, whether with municipals, treasuries or corporates, is little more than a bookkeeping technique, since no actual capital loss is involved. When interest rates go down, the new bonds (along with the old ones) will appreciate to where they were when purchased or will perhaps even go to a premium. In any event, they will certainly return the same principal at maturity. If you swap to comparable issues, you will not jeopardize your tax-exempt income or take on any additional risk.

Y · O · U · R   M · O · V · E

Second only to Treasury obligations in safety, municipal bonds have the added benefit of total tax exemption—at least for those individuals who are not subject to the alternative minimum tax. They are an excellent investment for either current tax-free income or for building a retirement account.

- If municipal bonds are to be profitable to you, you must know your personal income tax bracket, the coupon rate of the bonds, and the equivalent return on taxable bonds on an after-tax basis. Since municipal bond yields are less than other bonds, they are most advantageous for high-income earners, especially those in the 31 percent bracket. A 6 percent yield for someone in the 15 percent tax bracket makes no sense: If the investor can obtain 9 percent in other comparable investments, after taxes it is worth 7.65 percent. In short, sometimes it is better to pay the tax.

- If municipal bonds are to be bought, make sure that they indeed are totally tax-free. Bear in mind that there are now some municipals (private activity bonds and non-governmental purpose bonds) that yield a bit more, but do not qualify for complete tax exemption.

- If you require a guarantee on your funds, look for special bonds that provide additional security, such as insurance. But also be aware that such features come at the expense of yield—you may receive somewhat less return on your money than with uninsured bonds.

- If you do not have time to analyze each bond issue, and most investors do not, be guided by the credit ratings of the statistical services. As a rule, avoid nonrated bonds, regardless of how appealing you find the story behind the issue.

- If you buy premium bonds, remember that your current coupon yield is not your true return since there will be some capital depreciation as the bond matures.

- If you are going to swap (and it is a good idea to review bond holdings every quarter), try to switch to comparable coupon, rating and maturity. Do not trade from a discount to a premium, but try to find equivalent prices.

S·H·O·R·T·C·U·T

Municipal Bond Funds

- Dreyfus Tax-Exempt Bond Fund
- Federated Tax-Free Income Fund
- Fidelity Tax-Free High Yield
- John Hancock Tax-Exempt Income
- SteinRoe High-Yield Municipals
- T. Rowe Price Tax-Free Income Fund

• 7 •

Corporate Bonds

HIGH YIELD, SOME RISK

The industrial base of America rests as much on corporate bonds as it does on stocks. Bonds appeal to individuals and institutions that prefer to *lend* their funds to corporations rather than be partial owners. Bondholders become creditors of the corporation, and like the owners, they hope that the enterprise in which they placed their funds succeeds.

However, that does not mean that their interests are identical. When the economic weather turns stormy, conflicts often arise between the two. If you are thinking of investing in corporate bonds, it is important to understand the legal composition of the corporation and the kind of protection it will afford you.

For simplicity's sake we shall discuss only the major bond categories, but be aware that there are infinite variations. If you are going to be a long-term bondholder, you need only familiarize yourself with the introductory summaries (description, risk and ratings, maturity and duration, income and yield, special benefits). On the other hand, if you anticipate trading and taking advantage of swings in interest rates, the whole chapter will provide you with additional information for short-term investing.

Description

Corporate bonds represent a form of debt that may be *secured* or *unsecured*. The strongest public corporations—the AT&Ts, GMs and Exxons in the United States—can borrow money on their good name alone. Thus, their bonds are unsecured. Because lenders believe that they will be paid back with interest by these first-class corporations, there is no need to demand security or collateral. These unsecured bond issues are called *debentures*. Holders of debentures have all the rights of general creditors—a claim to the corporations assets that is superior to the claims of the stockholders.

A corporation may also issue *subordinate debentures,* a weaker unsecured issue that comes after the debenture-holder's claim on assets. They frequently pay higher interest rates than full debentures. Moreover, they often offer the bondholder the right to convert these subordinate debentures into common stock.

By contrast, mortgage bonds are secured by some form of collateral. Mortgage bonds reflect specific liens on corporate property. Companies that have limited or no physical properties to back their bonds can use the assets they do have (such as subsidiary companies, or their holdings of stocks and bonds of other companies) as collateral for the bonds they issue. Hence these bond issues are called *collateralized trust bonds*.

Finally, airlines, railroads and other transportation companies borrow through an independent trustee, who buys the equipment (planes, barges or rolling stock) and issues *equipment trust certificates* to pay the manufacturer of the equipment. The railroads or airlines repay their debt by entering into a lease arrangement with the trustee for the equipment; once the debt is fully paid off, they take ownership of the equipment.

The rent paid by the transportation company to the trustee is passed through to the owners of the certificates in the form of interest and principal. Equipment trust certificates have an excellent credit history because of the ease with which the equipment can be sold off if necessary to repay the debt. In fact, in poor economic times transportation companies will pay off the certificate holders before the bondholders.

Corporate bonds are typically sold in $1,000 denominations. They generally pay a fixed rate of interest semiannually and are now usually sold at or about face value in registered form, though many bearer bonds are still on the scene. The contract that explains the nature of the bond is called the *bond indenture*. A trustee, usually a bank or trust company, acts as the fiduciary for the bondholders, going to court if necessary to protect their legal rights as spelled out in the indenture.

Risk and Rating

As senior securities, bonds are generally considered safer than the common stock of a corporation. Nevertheless, bonds do have some risk: If the corporation cannot pay its interest on the bonds, the price of the bonds will fall in value. If that situation is temporary and the company is restored to financial health, the bonds will resume paying interest (and the accumulated defaulted interest, though that may depend on the specifics as spelled out in the indenture). If the situation results in bankruptcy, the bondholders as creditors will be paid from the remaining assets of the bankrupt corporation.

In any event, prices of bonds do fluctuate to reflect the condition of the business. This market risk can be reduced by buying quality bond issues. Corporate creditworthiness is measured by the rating agencies. These ratings are extremely important to the bond market and largely determine the price at which these securities trade.

Financial service companies rate bonds. For example the highest rating—AAA and AA—might be given to high-grade bonds; medium-grade bonds could be rated A and BBB; speculative bonds could get BB and B; those in default could get CCC, CC, C and D. (A more detailed explanation of the ratings appears later in this chapter.)

Finally, corporate bonds are subject to interest rate risk, moving up and down inversely to current interest rate moves.

Maturity and Duration

Most corporate bond issues mature between 5 and 20 years. If these bonds have an early call provision, the company may decide to redeem an issue early if interest rates are favorable. Some bonds have sinking fund provisions, which retire some part of the principal before maturity. Such bonds may be paid off at par or sometimes at a small premium above par. Whatever the circumstance, called bonds rarely bring good news to the bondholder, since the issuer is likely to be retiring high-interest issues in a lower-interest rate climate.

The bondholder is then left with proceeds that must be reinvested in a low interest-rate environment. Try to buy bonds with some protection against early calls. This is most likely in shorter-term notes and bonds, which may not be callable until the bond reaches its maturity date.

Income and Yield

Corporate bonds offer higher yields than Treasury issues or municipal bonds. The reason is simple: They carry a higher risk of default, since there is no governmental safety net. Moreover, they are obliged to pay more for borrowed money since the income to the bondholder is taxable. The yield on a new bond is fixed by the coupon rate. If you buy a bond above or below par, the current yield can be calculated by dividing the annual amount of interest (the coupon rate) by the amount you paid for the bond. For example, if you purchase the AT&T 6% of 2,000 for 81, you will receive $60 per bond. The current yield is:

$$\frac{\$60}{\$810} = 7.41\%$$

Calculate the yield to maturity to see what the return on your money will be after adjusting for the discount or premium that was in the purchase price. (For additional information on yield, see Chapter 2.)

Special Benefits

The income you receive from corporate bonds is taxable unless the bonds are held in tax-advantaged accounts (such as an individual retirement account).

THE CORPORATE WORLD

The issuing of corporate bonds is initiated by a public company because it either no longer wishes to issue more stock or it wants to reduce its reliance on bank loans through this cheaper form of financing. It is cheaper to borrow from the public at fixed rates than from banks, with their variable rates tied to the prime lending rate.

The company hires an investment banking firm to underwrite the issue and comply with all the requirements of the law and the regulations of the SEC. A trust indenture spells out the company's obligations and appoints a trustee to look out for the investors' interests. The investment banker then issues a prospectus to potential investors, highlighting the terms of the deal—the coupon or interest rate, the price and/or par value, the possibility of an early call, the maturity date, and any other key features that must be identified in the name of full disclosure.

All corporate bonds must be registered with the SEC and with the various states in which they will be sold (termed "blue skyed" to be sure that citizens are not buying a piece of the heavens). It should be clear that the act of registration, whether in stocks or bonds, does *not* give an official certification of investment quality. Rainmakers could sell bonds in their business as long as they disclosed the true nature and relevant facts in promising precipitation.

There are a number of different ways of underwriting a bond issue. The corporation's investment bankers form a syndicate with other like firms to underwrite the bonds and sell them to the public. When members of the syndicate deal as principals, they buy the whole corporate issue and take on the responsibility of selling it, retaining what cannot be sold. Or the syndicate may act as an agent, taking a commission for a best efforts commitment. Some syndicates will attempt to sell an issue of an unknown company on an all-or-none basis. Finally, if a company is new or highly speculative, it may attempt to handle the underwriting of the bond issue itself.

It makes sense to buy corporate bonds from the underwriters, since the bonds are issued without any commission fees. A notice, called a "tombstone," of the offering will be published in the financial press (see Figure 7.1). However, many corporate issues are presold and the tombstone appears as a matter of record only. If you are interested in buying original corporate issues, you should read S&P's *Creditwatch* or Moody's *Bond Survey*; both list upcoming financing.

Depending on the popularity of the issues, underwriters may attempt to stabilize the market by actively intervening in the aftermarket for a short period. But once the distribution is complete, corporate bonds are traded in the secondary markets—largely in the over-the-counter market.

BUYING AND SELLING BONDS

To buy corporate bonds in the secondary market, you have to deal with a retail broker. You can purchase bonds from full-service retail brokers or from the discounters. (For additional information about selecting a broker, see *The Basics of Investing,* Chapter 9.)

Perhaps it makes less difference which kind of broker you use, since commission fees on bonds are not only quite small, but competitive. In general, they are about $5 per bond.

You can, of course, place an order for a specific issue or you can express your interest in a generic issue—for example, in a AAA utility company or industrial, maturing in seven years with a coupon of 6 to 7 percent, and a yield to maturity of 8 to 9 percent. The broker will search the firm's inventory or the list of over-the-counter bonds and attempt to find something comparable.

In the financial pages of your newspaper, you will find a listing of issues traded on the New York Stock Exchange, the American Stock Exchange and the over-the-counter market. For example, if you were interested in AT&T 6 percent of 2,000, you would find in the bond table:

FIGURE 7.1   Sample Tombstone

This announcement is under no circumstance to be
construed as an offer to sell or a solicitation of an offer to
buy any of these securities. The offering is made only by
the Prospectus.

New Issue   **October 1, 1991**
$100,000,000
ABC CORPORATION
General Mortgage Bonds
Price 99.646

Copies of the Prospectus may be obtained in any State
or jurisdiction in which this announcement is circulated
from only such of the undersigned or other dealers or
brokers as may be lawfully offer these securities in such
State or jurisdiction.

1st Investment Bankers, Inc.   Doe Securities & Co.
Bull, Bear & Sons Corporation

Bonds	Current Yld	Vol	Close	Net Change
AT&T 6s00	7.4	79	81	3/4

This entry shows that AT&T has an issue of bonds with
a coupon rate of 6 percent which mature in 2,000. The
current yield is the coupon rate, (6 percent) divided by the
price (81). The price is quoted as a percentage of par (face
value) which is usually $1,000: therefore, the actual price
is $810 and the current yield is ($60 ÷ 810) 7.4 percent.

Volume is expressed in thousands. In this case, 79
$1,000 bonds were traded for the day, an increase in value
of $7.50 per bond. Bear in mind that a point in the bond
market is ten dollars, not one dollar as in the stock market.
Table 7.1 shows the dollar equivalents for fractions.

If the common stock is trading at or above the conversion price, the convertible will act like a stock. When the common stock is trading below the conversion price, the convertible acts increasingly like a pure bond. A glance at the bond tables will reveal that some bonds are traded flat (f), a notation that indicates the company is not presently paying interest on this issue. When traded, there will be no accumulated interest to account for from the new owner.

The practice in the bond world is to pay the seller of the bond the interest that accumulated from the last coupon payment date through the day before the delivery date. After all, it is only equitable for the owner of the instrument to earn the interest. In the case of the AT&T 6s of 00, the buyer would pay $15 to the seller if the bond was transferred in the middle of the semiannual payment period ($60 ÷ 4 = $15).

The formula for calculating the exact accrued interest is:

$$\text{Annual interest} \times \frac{\text{Days held}}{360 \text{ days}}$$

$$\$60 \times \frac{90}{360} = \$15$$

If the buyer wants to know the yield to maturity of the AT&T bond, the formula (as explained in Appendix A) is:

$$\frac{\text{Coupon rate} + \text{Average yearly discount}}{(\text{Par value} + \text{Purchase price}) \div 2}$$

$$\frac{60 + 19}{(1{,}000 + 810) \div 2} = 8.73\%$$

You should know one other additional piece of information before buying a bond: The yearly or 52-week price

TABLE 7.1   Decimal Equivalents for Bond Fractions

1/8	=	$ 1.25
2/8	=	$ 2.50
3/8	=	$ 3.75
4/8	=	$ 5.00
5/8	=	$ 6.25
6/8	=	$ 7.50
7/8	=	$ 8.75
8/8	=	$10.00

range. Daily newspapers have, for the most part, stopped listing this information, but it can be found in the weekly summary in magazines such as *Barron's* or in S&P's *Bond Guide*. In this case, the AT&T bond traded between a high of 83 3/4 ($837.50) and a low of 73 7/8 ($738.75).

PRICING

Like so many things in life, what you see is not necessarily what you get, especially if you are dealing in small quantities of bonds, say five or ten. You are likely to be asked to take a concession from the printed price. In general, prices on bonds tend to fluctuate less than stock prices.

The best prices, those that have the smallest spread between bid (what the dealer will buy for) and the offered (what the dealer will sell for) are the most actively traded bonds. In most cases, the spread is 1/4 ($2.50) or 1/2 ($5.00) point. For inactive bonds, ones from small issues or little known companies, the spread may widen considerably, from one to three points.

If your strategy is to buy and hold, the dealer's spread may not be a consideration. However, if you want to take advantage of swings in the market because of interest rate moves, you will find that large spreads make trading unprofitable.

At the very least, large spreads in unknown issues can reduce the yield. For example, if you buy five bonds at the initial offering with an 8 percent coupon, you will earn $80 per bond. Suppose a year later you decide to sell the bonds at par, since interest rates have remained stable. But now you must consider the commission charge, one-half to one full point per bond.

In short, you might find an average cost of one to two full points to trade out, thus lowering your effective yield to $70 (7 percent) or $60 (6 percent). This is one of the reasons that small investors buy and hold bonds for many years to spread out the selling costs. If the bonds are held to maturity or to call they are redeemed free of charge. If you intend to trade, it is worthwhile to stay with the most liquid bonds, the ones that have instant marketability.

RATINGS: A MATTER OF QUALITY

While interest rates affect bonds prices, so too do the ratings assigned them by the financial statistical services. New bonds are issued with a quality rating already affixed. This gives a prospective buyer an instant understanding of the issuer's creditworthiness. It is too complicated to analyze how the services arrive at their ratings, but they are taken extremely seriously by professional money managers. The ratings are based on a series of factors and ratios considered highly important in evaluating debt instruments, including the following:

- The amount of previously issued debt.
- The position of the industry and the stability of the company's business.

- The quality of the company's cash flow and its ability to service its debt and other obligations.
- The executive abilities of management.

Specifically, the rating services pay special attention to interest coverage, that is, the number of times net income (before interest and taxes) covers the company's charges. Thus, the following ratio represents interest coverage:

$$\frac{\text{Annual interest charges} + \text{Net income}}{\text{Annual interest charges}} = \text{Interest coverage}$$

For example, one of the largest retail close-out chains had annual interest income of $7 million, net income of $13 million, a ratio of 2.85. This coverage was considered weak by the rating agencies. The following year, its interest costs were about the same, but a large increase in income raised the interest coverage to 3.9, a healthier position.

Many analysts are comfortable only when coverage is four or five times. However, in recent years with the increase of leverage and debt throughout the corporate world, the ratio has fallen. Clearly, a trend of less and less coverage is worrisome.

Another test is the current ratio:

$$\frac{\text{Current assets}}{\text{Current liabilities}}$$

This should be at least 2 for most industries. A more stringent measure is the quick ratio:

$$\frac{\text{Current assets} - \text{Inventories}}{\text{Current liabilities}}$$

This ratio should be at least *1*. Both ratios attempt to measure the value of a company's working capital position and to see if it is healthy.

Finally, another guide to creditworthiness is the simple debt-to-equity ratio. Once a corporation takes on more than 25 percent of its capitalization in debt, it is on its way to the slippery slope. (Some industries—utilities and banks—are capital-intensive businesses and are an exception to this rule. They normally use a great deal of borrowed money to finance their operations.) At 50 percent, the company should be considered highly leveraged, and generally avoided for safety's sake.

If you are going to invest in bonds, you should be aware of these ratios (among others) to determine the creditworthiness of the corporate issuer. The relevant information can be found in the balance sheets and income statements published in the corporate annual report, as well as in secondary sources issued by the financial services. (For a more detailed explanation of the key ratios and measurements of profitability, growth, liquidity and credit see *The Basics of Stocks,* Chapter 4.)

Many investors simply rely on the evaluations and ratings of rating services. At the very least, the following criteria give you general guidelines:

Corporate Bond Evaluations

- **AAA** is the highest rating assigned to a bond. It indicates that the issuer's capacity to pay interest and repay principal is extremely strong.
- **AA** issues differ from the top-rates securities only by a small degree. This rating indicates a very strong capacity to pay interest and repay principal.
- **A** issues are somewhat more susceptible to changes in economic conditions than debt in higher-rated catego-

ries. However, the issuer has a strong capacity to pay interest and repay principal.

- **BBB** debt issuers have adequate capacity to pay interest payments and repay principal. Adverse economic conditions are more likely to weaken the issuer's capacity to pay interest and repay principal.
- **BB, B, CCC** and **CC** debt is regarded as predominantly speculative with respect to capacity to pay interest and repay principal. BB indicates the lowest degree of speculation and CC the highest. While such obligations may have some protective characteristics, these considerations are outweighed by exposure to adverse conditions.
- **C** ratings are reserved for *income bonds* (bonds that pay interest only if it is earned by the corporation) on which no interest is being paid.
- **D** ratings indicate that the issuer is in default, and payment of interest or repayment of principal, or both, is in arrears.

The ratings from AA to B may be modified by the addition of a plus or minus sign to show relative standing within the major rating categories.

How these ratings affect bond prices is difficult to pinpoint. However, for two corporate bonds of comparable coupon rates and maturity dates, there may well be a difference of 25 basis points (1/4 of 1 percent) in yield between AAA and AA. Late in 1991 the Standard & Poor's index of industrial bond yields showed these differences:

Industrials	Percent
AAA	8.67
AA	8.98
A	9.44

BBB	9.84
BB	11.73
B	14.31

For comparison's sake, at the same time other key market interest rates were as follows:

Three-month Treasury bills	5.45
Thirty-year Treasury bonds	7.95
Money market funds	5.34
Prime lending rate	8.50
Dow Jones Industrial Average stocks (dividend)	3.33

While a relationship exists between bond yields and interest rates, there is no simple ratio: At most times, the difference between three-month Treasury securities and long-term bonds is 200 to 300 basis points.

ENTER EVENT RISK

Prices are largely determined by these ratings—a fact underscored when one of the major rating services upgrades or downgrades the rating of a bond issue. The next day, the issue's price may be up or down a couple of points. These revisions usually occur because of some slow erosion of investment characteristics. On occasion, bonds are also subject to "event risk," a relatively new element in the fixed-income world. Of late, the rapid restructuring of corporations through mergers and acquisitions or leveraged buyouts has put bonds in jeopardy overnight.

You cannot simply assume that because bonds are senior securities, that they are the general creditors, that these obligations represent total security. Bonds, of whatever kind, represent a financing technique—the corporation may be in less than ideal health. Moreover, even issues of healthy corporations may have sinking spells.

Indeed, new and subsequent financing arrangements may turn older, quality issues into something less than that. With the advent of "junk" bond financing in management reorganizations or hostile leveraged buyouts, the target company's earlier bond issues are trashed when it becomes apparent that the new corporate balance sheet will be loaded down with onerous debt.

If the corporation loses its fight to remain independent, it may be absorbed into a corporation with lower ratings; if it wins the battle, it may have sold off some key assets (known as the "crown jewels") to defend itself or have bought back large portion of its equity at inflated prices. In either case, the event further weakens the corporation and adds to its debt.

When the RJR Nabisco leveraged buyout was announced, good quality corporate issues of the company declined in price by nearly 20 percent overnight. The market was clearly concerned about the dilution and downgrading of assets. That change in perception and fall in price constituted an enormous loss to bondholders who had recently bought what they thought were top quality nonspeculative obligations.

Whether it is a threat of a takeover or the actual tender for a company, the replacement of the common stockholders with high-yielding ("junk") bonds so dramatically alters the investment safeguards of the older bonds that the market downgrades their prices long before the rating agencies have had time to consider the new arrangements.

The effect can be devastating, with losses of 10 or 20 percent of a bond's value. The RJR Nabisco takeover was perhaps the most flagrant case, followed by litigation from institutional bondholders. For the individual investor, there was a subsequent flight from corporate bonds to government securities. New bond issues now have protective covenants or *put* features (the right to return the bonds to the issuer for a refund) that attempt to protect the bond-holder from event risk.

AT A DISCOUNT

An investor can look at a listing of corporate bonds and find some issues selling at great discounts for causes other than event risk devaluations. These discounts are offered for one of two reasons. Prices of low coupon bonds naturally fell when interest rates rose. These bonds are at a deep discount (under 70) because of interest rate pressures or market forces.

However, the second group of bonds was originally issued at deep discounts, far below par, since the coupon rate is far less than the current yield to maturity in the market place. Thus both are sold at discounts; the former did not start out that way, while the latter did.

An original-issue deep discount bond might be issued at 55 with a 6 percent coupon and have a yield to maturity of 14.5 percent. If you want current income, this issue would not fit your needs. On the other hand, if you want a high yield to maturity, it certainly would. The issue would keep your current tax low since the interest paid was relatively low. However, the annual incremental growth of the bond is taxable. The original issue discount is taxed by the IRS—a taxpayer has to amortize the discount over the issue's life.

Y•O•U•R   M•O•V•E

- If you are considering investing in corporate securities, you should decide whether you want to be a long-term holder or a short-term trader. If you are planning a long-term commitment to these high-yielding instruments—by and large, they yield more than any other category of bonds—you must answer another question. Do you want high current income or a high yield to maturity?

- If you opt for high current income (regardless of the tax consequences), you must select either a new issue with a high coupon rate or one in the secondary market. In the former case, you pay no commission, you know exactly the coupon rate, the yield to maturity, the rating and who has underwritten the issue. If you buy in the secondary market, you will have to calculate yield to maturity, research the rating, the terms of the issue, and history of its price action.

- As a long-term investor, you have to make only one timely commitment. You must buy new or available issues at the appropriate time, usually when prevailing rates are high. A double-digit yield is desirable, since the average return on bonds is only the inflation rate, plus 3 percent. Since 1983 the inflation rate has been about 4.5 percent per year.

- As a short-term investor, you must continually make interest-rate decisions to be profitable. While there are a number of different strategies, primarily you must buy bonds when rates are very high and the prices are low, hold them while yields come down, and then watch bond prices advance. Yields are only signposts to traders, not ends in themselves. Because of the large numbers of dollars involved, the need to have current information and the wide swing corporate bonds can take, short-term trading is not recommended to individual, nonprofessional investors. Today, most bond traders use bond futures contracts to anticipate interest rate moves or to hedge an underlying fixed-income portfolio. (Bond futures are described in *The Basics of Speculating*.)

S • H • O • R • T • C • U • T

Corporate Bond Funds

- Axe-Houghton Income Fund
- Cigna Income Fund
- Kemper Income & Capital Preservation
- Scudder Income Fund
- Vanguard Fixed Income—Investment Grade
- Wasatch Income

• 8 •

Convertible Bonds

THE BEST OF BOTH WORLDS

Is it possible to have the best of both the bond market and the stock market? Convertible bonds attempt to answer the question positively. They are hybrid securities that appeal to both fear and greed, the two emotions that dominate the investment world.

They have a place in your portfolio if you require a return on your funds (at least comparable in many instances to what you might get in a savings bank) while maintaining a potential position in the stock market. Convertibles offer the relative stability of bonds and the potential capital appreciation of shares.

Corporations issue convertibles to increase their capital without immediately diluting the common stock. The eventual exchange of the convertible bond into shares will dilute the equity, but that will not happen until later. In the first place, convertible bonds supply the corporation relatively cheap capital. Convertibles have coupon rates that are lower than the interest rates necessary to float their straight corporate bonds, since the sweetener or enticement is the conversion privilege.

On the other hand, the yield is higher than the return from the dividends of the common stock. If the common stock appreciates, the convertible holder can exercise the option to obtain what amounts to cheap stock—stock far below the market value.

Risk and Ratings

Convertible bonds are subject to interest rate risk. That is, they can be hurt if prevailing interest rates move up sharply, far above the coupon rate. They are less likely to be affected if the underlying corporation hits a patch of bad weather.

Some investors view convertibles negatively. They contend that these hybrid securities give you not the best of both worlds, but the worst. You do not receive the higher yields associated with the senior bonds, and you do not fully participate in the advances in price when the company is highly successful. Therefore, they suggest, you are taking on more risk rather than less.

However, this tradeoff appeals to many investors who wish to combine some of the safety inherent in debt obligations (if only subordinated debt) with the chance to convert to appreciating stock. Regardless of how you look at this tradeoff, convertibles are considered to be riskier than other forms of fixed-income securities (except perhaps for junk bonds) since their prices fluctuate more than straight bonds.

Convertible bonds are rated in the same manner as straight bonds. (See the chapter on corporate bonds for an explanation of ratings.) Many convertibles lack an investment quality rating, that is, they do not have the financial qualifications to be categorized in the top four rankings. Nevertheless, there are hundreds of convertible bond issues and some do indeed meet investment-grade criteria.

Maturity and Duration

Convertible bonds are originally issued with a maturity date, the time when the issue will be redeemed by the corporation. However, the conversion privilege may or may not last the life of the bond. You must check to see when the conversion issue expires—in a minority of cases, it ends long before the maturity date.

You must also check to see if the convertible has a call provision. The issuer may exercise this privilege to force conversion. It is in your interest to buy bonds which give you protection against a premature call.

Income and Yield

These bonds pay interest semiannually at the stated coupon rate. Thus a 6 percent coupon will pay $300 twice a year. To determine the current yield, you must divide the coupon rate by the market price. If the bond was selling for 120 ($1,200), the current yield would be 5 percent. The yield to maturity is calculated the same way as straight bonds, but that figure may be academic since the purpose of buying convertibles is to convert them before the maturity date.

For comparison's sake, Champion International was paying $1.10 per share dividend, a yield of 3.4 percent when the stock was selling at $32. The company also had an issue of 9.5 percent debentures of 2016, selling at 90 ($900) for a current yield of 10.5 percent. Between both was an issue of convertible bonds, 6.5 percent of 2011 selling at 100 ($1,000) for a current yield of 6.5 percent. This spread is typical for corporations that have this range of investment securities.

Special Benefits

Interest income and capital gains are taxed in the ordinary way for individuals, unless the convertible bonds are held in a tax-deferred account. Conversion of bonds to common stock is not considered a taxable event, in other words there is no gain or loss for tax purposes.

THE CASE FOR CONVERTIBLES

Investors like convertible bonds because of their dual nature. They are especially attractive when markets are trendless or nervous. They bring in a relatively decent return while providing the potential for capital gains if the stock market turns aggressively positive. Therefore, it is important to appreciate that convertibles are first of all debt instruments and must be analyzed as such.

To determine what they are worth, you must ask: At what price would this issue trade, considering the coupon rate, the credit rating and the maturity? These elements give a convertible bond its *investment value,* or its intrinsic value. This can easily be found by comparing similar straight bonds.

For example, assume the convertible bond has a coupon of 7.5 percent and a maturity of ten years, while a straight bond of similar characteristics pays 11 percent: both are priced at par ($1,000). Since long-term interest rates are about 11 percent, at what price would the convertible have to sell at to yield not 7.5 percent, but 11 percent?

By consulting bond tables or a calculator, you would find that the convertible had to sell at a discount, $790. The intrinsic value of the convertible is $790, not the $1,000 face value. In other words, under the most adverse circumstances, the convertible will sell only on its investment value. It does not sell at only its investment value because of the added value which comes from its conversion privileges.

This privilege, or *conversion ratio,* is stated in the issue's indenture and is fixed for the life of the bond. The conversion ratio (for example, 40 shares per bond) is usually set well above the current market price.

If the common stock is selling at $15 per share, the conversion price is $25—a $1,000 bond would realize 40 shares ($1,000 ÷ 25). In other words, if you bought the new convertible bond at $1,000, you could convert the bond to 40 shares of common stock at any time. Obviously, you would convert only when it becomes worthwhile.

You would not convert your bond into 40 shares if the price of the shares was less than $25. If the stock was selling at $15, the equivalent value of 40 shares would be $600. Clearly, nothing is to be gained at an exchange below the conversion price.

In cases such as this, when the convertible's price is substantially above the value of the underlying common, the bond's yield is likely to be in line with comparable straight (nonconvertible) bonds. Such convertibles do not respond much to changes in the price of the company's common stock. Instead, they rise and fall in accordance with fluctuations of interest rates and changes in the companies' financial condition.

The *conversion value* of a convertible bond is the number of shares of common into which the bond is convertible times the market price per share of the common stock. Thus, if the price moves to $20 per share, the conversion value would be $800 ($20 × 40 shares). Conversion value is directly related to market price, increasing in lockstep.

If the price of the common falls, the bond will decline, but only to its investment value. It will then act increasingly like a straight bond.

Convertibles do not sell below or at a discount to its conversion value, since investors would buy the bonds and convert them into the higher priced stocks. When the stock price goes up, the conversion feature takes on increasing value until it reaches the conversion price ($25). At this point, the conversion value of the bond is $1,000. If the underlying factors for the company are bullish, then the bond may well sell above its conversion value, at a premium.

If the common advances further, the convertible bond will sell at a premium over conversion value. This is often expressed as a percentage of the conversion value. If the price of the shares moved to $35, the market value of the convertible would be ($35 × 40) $1,400. Since the conversion value (known also as the *conversion parity*) was $1,000 ($25 × 40), the premium is $1,400 minus $1,000, divided by $1,000—a premium of 40 percent.

A CALL ON THE COMMON

From these elements, you can draw some conclusions. Convertibles place a floor for downside risk with their investment value. There is no ceiling, since the potential for the common stock is theoretically unlimited.

When the stock price falls, the convertible will also decline and act more like a straight bond as it reaches its investment value. When the bond is trading at or above the parity of conversion value, the bond tends to act increasingly like the stock. If you are an equity holder, you might consider selling the stock at that point to buy the convertible, since it usually yields more than the dividends of the stock.

Convertibles are frequently subject to a call. The higher a convertible trades above its investment value, and then above its call price, the riskier it becomes.

If the issuing company so chooses, the convertible can be called for redemption—in some cases at prices below current market levels. An issue is more likely to be called if the coupon rate is higher than the cost of similar borrowing at the call date.

Since the conversion option remains open in the period from the announcement of the call to the date of redemption, the downside for the holder is limited to the premium—the difference between the bond's market price at the time of the call and the bond's value in common stock upon conversion.

Another element of risk has also entered the convertible market: Leveraged buyouts and takeovers have downgraded the quality of bonds. Convertibles trading at great premiums can be treated harshly in a corporate restructuring. That is one of the reasons for being wary of a convertible that has more than a 20 percent or 25 percent premium. These risks are somewhat softened because the convertibles will eventually be redeemed at par, regardless of what happens to the equity.

Convertible bonds are appropriate for some fixed-income investors wishing to stick a toe in the equity market. If you have no interest in the stock market, then you should avoid convertible bonds, since the yields on straight bonds are superior. If, on the other hand, some of your portfolio is invested in common stock, then convertible bonds are worth considering as a way of obtaining shares in desirable companies (without paying a broker's commission).

Remember that while the yields are not as high as a corporation's straight bonds, the return is often considerably better than the dividend of shares. However, convertible bonds can be adversely affected by rising interest rates and a tumble in the price of the common stock.

Y · O · U · R   M · O · V · E

- Buy convertible bonds only if you are interested in the common stock of the corporation. Convertibles appreciate at a slower rate than the common stock.
- You should like the company's prospects for it is only the appreciation of the shares that make it worthwhile to hold the convertibles. Convertibles yield more interest than the dividends of the common stock, but less than the interest from straight bonds.
- Try to buy convertibles whose conversion premium is small or negligible.
- Convertibles are perhaps best bought at the bottom of a business cycle when stock prices are depressed and bond yields are generally low. You then receive a yield almost equivalent to a new straight bond issue, plus a call on the common free of charge.

S · H · O · R · T · C · U · T

Convertible Bond Funds

- American Capital Convertible
- Bancroft Convertible
- Castle Convertible
- Ellsworth Convertible Growth and Income
- Lincoln National Convertible
- TCW Convertible Securities

• *9* •

High-Yielding Corporate Bonds

ALL ABOUT JUNK BONDS

The riskiest of all bonds are high-yielding corporate obligations commonly known as *junk bonds*. The return on your investment cannot be matched by any other type of bond. Interest rates of high-yielding corporate bonds exceed yields of AAA-rated corporate bonds by 300 to 600 basis points (3 to 6 percent).

There is a catch, of course: These bonds are exceedingly vulnerable to default. They are highly speculative securities. If you are a fixed-income investor relying on periodic interest payments, you should avoid this category of bonds. If you are concerned about the safety of your principal, you should also avoid these securities.

Junk bonds are debt securities of issuers with limited credit standing. In other words, the corporations that issue these bonds have either no credit history because they are relatively new, or a credit history with serious problems of one sort or another. Do you really want to trust these marginal businesses with your hard-earned dollars?

Risk and Rating

The nickname tells all: High risk is inherent in high-yield bonds. Nevertheless, your portfolio may well have a place for some of these securities if you are not risk-averse. While you should not structure a retirement portfolio around junk bonds, some fractional percentage of them will raise the return for your portfolio as a whole.

In general, they fall into the category of "business-person's risk," that is, the kind of risk an aggressive investor with substantial earnings might undertake. The rating agencies play an active role in grading these issues—usually at BB or lower.

Maturity and Duration

Junk bonds tend to be shorter in duration than investment-grade bonds. When junk bonds are used to finance a *leveraged buyout,* it is typically assumed that such financing will be needed for only five to ten years.

There is usually a minefield of conditions as to when junk bonds are callable. Be sure to look for some elements of protection in the bond prospectus. For example, the company may be prohibited from paying dividends or buying in its own stock. It is also important to see if the covenant prohibits the corporation from selling all its assets, leaving an indebted shell behind. Many issues have no call protection, and are indeed called early or exchanged for other securities.

Income and Yield

Junk bonds return about 5 percent to 7 percent more than long-term Treasuries. This ratio is often regarded as a key to whether the bonds are underpriced or overpriced in relation to the market. In a period of uncertainty, investors' "flight to quality" pushes the spread between junk bonds and Treasuries even further as junk prices drop and yields rise—the opposite of what happen to Treasury securities.

The rich yields are not for the risk-averse—some say that they are only for speculators. If you are tempted, diversification will reduce exposure to untoward events. Stay away from small issues, since these may be hard to sell should the need arise. A number of high-yielding mutual funds provide diversification for investors who wish to invest some of their funds for higher returns.

A number of issues do not pay interest but promise to pay the investor shares of common stock. These payment-in-kind junk bonds are only for the truly adventurous.

Special Benefits

Since junk bonds are taxable investments and are expected to provide more income, they will naturally be subject to higher taxes. However, in a tax-advantaged account, they look spectacular: For someone in a 28 percent tax bracket, a 15 percent bond will produce an untaxed 20.8 percent. Taxes will have to be paid when the proceeds are withdrawn, but then presumably at a lower tax rate.

THE BRAVE NEW WORLD OF JUNK BONDS

There have always been high-yielding bonds, those that yielded far higher returns than investment-grade corporate bonds. They didn't start out that way, but were subsequently priced at a deep discount because of their poor financial condition. There was one drawback to those high-yielding bonds: The companies that had issued them (usually at par, $1,000) had usually fallen on hard times. They were still paying the interest, but the marketplace took a dreary view of their prospects and so marked the price of those bonds down—often far down.

Thus, if the original coupon rate was 7.5 percent, the yield was about 15 percent when the price of the bonds had fallen in half (to $500). Naturally, they appealed to gamblers and speculators. The adventuresome could buy them for their high yields, but there was also the possibility of appreciation in value. If the company worked out its problems, the bonds would rise in price and provide a sizable capital gain. So much for history.

In the early Eighties, an investment banking house, Drexel Burnham Lambert, devised a financing technique to provide funds for companies whose credit ratings were less than sterling. In fact, the nature of their balance sheets indicated that they would *not* qualify for investment grade status—the top four ratings, AAA, AA, A and BBB. There was grave doubt as to whether they could pay the interest on the debt, as well as the principal, in good or bad economic weather. The companies were either too small, too weakly capitalized, too unprofitable or too indebted to qualify for investment grade status.

Drexel found that there was an untapped market for high-yield bonds. Banks had been an alternate source of corporate borrowing, and in the late Seventies and early Eighties banks were busy lending their available credit to Third World underdeveloped nations, the oil industry and farming. Small and medium-sized companies had long felt left out of the financial loop as larger and better-known companies absorbed most of the available credit.

It was this vacuum that Drexel exploited. Since less than 4 percent of all American corporations were considered to be of investment quality, there was plenty of room to sell high-yield corporate bonds. And as the Eighties commenced, there was an increased use of debt. The use of large amounts of borrowed funds became a respectable way to finance corporate needs. For many small and medium-size companies, the objective was no longer to have spotless credit credentials, but to maximize corporate borrowings and in turn maximize corporate earnings. High-yielding bonds became an immediate and huge success.

From the investor's point of view, junk bonds were just what the doctor ordered. Yields as high as 12, 14 and 16 percent were not uncommon and institutions and private individuals thought they had gone to heaven without passing over. For the Eighties, junk bond buyers had their cake and were eating it as well.

However, junk bonds were part and parcel of the longest peacetime business expansion in the United States in the Eighties. The public junk bond market grew exponentially, approaching $200 billion with about 1,000 companies participating. They remained untested in a recession.

In the fall of 1989, the junk bond market was severely tested when a number of proposed leveraged buyouts fell through. The commercial banks and other institutional investors abruptly stopped financing the megadeals, mergers and corporate restructuring because of the October 1989 mini-crash when the Dow Jones Industrial Average fell 190 points in one day. As credit dried up, the junk bond market fell apart. Prices declined dramatically and some issues could not be traded at all.

It also became apparent that an increasing number of junk bond issuers were defaulting on their interest payments. As business slowed down at the end of the expansion, it was impossible to cover the high interest charges associated with the high-yield bonds.

Reports throughout the Eighties indicated that the default rate on junk bonds was rather low, perhaps only 2 percent. While this was ten times higher than the default rate of investment-grade bonds, it was acceptable to many investors.

At the beginning of 1990, the most comprehensive report on junk bonds was released by the Bond Investors Association. It concluded that the default rate in the junk bond market (both public and private issues) was 38 percent for any given year. In other words, the study found that over the life of 3,500 bond issues representing $300 billion, a full 38 percent would either default on their payment of interest, have an early redemption or exchange the bonds for other issues because of imminent default.

Another great blow to the high-yielding bond market was the bankruptcy of Drexel Burnham Lambert, the firm that started it all, in February, 1990. While the short-term prospects for the "junk" bond market after Drexel's collapse were not good, the long-term considerations remain positive. Too many American corporations that need capital do not have investment-grade credentials. Therefore, some form of high-yielding bonds are likely to remain a part of the investment scene for such corporations requiring credit.

If you are seriously considering high-yield securities, you now have a yardstick: Almost four out of ten junk bond issues seem destined to have serious problems. For the individual investor, even the risk-loving investor, this is not just a chancy investment, it is more like a game of Russian roulette.

Nevertheless, if you wish to raise your return on some portion of your portfolio, high-yield securities will assist you to that end. It would be folly for a fixed-income investor to place more than a small fraction of his or her funds in such bonds—perhaps 5 or 10 percent. If you are seriously considering junk bonds and can tolerate their high risk, you should be prepared to lose some portion of your capital. A loss of capital will, of course, reduce your return, perhaps even give you a negative return if a number of issues in your portfolio do default.

The only way an investor should participate in this market is by diversifying. A selection of at least half a dozen issues will afford you some protection. Better still, if the high risk does not deter you, a high-yield mutual fund will give you professional management in a treacherous market. In addition, it can buy and sell these bonds without the concession in price associated with trades of a few securities.

Y•O•U•R   M•O•V•E

- Consider your risk quotient. If the real possibility of the loss of some of your investment funds is unacceptable, stay away from high-yielding bonds.

- If you can accept the risk associated with junk bonds, remember that the higher the return, the more likely the case for default. Businesses (especially ones with inordinate amount of debt) cannot withstand an upward ratchet of interest charges if interest rates move up, nor can they cover their service charges if the economy slows down. If you reach for the very highest return, you are positioning yourself exceedingly close to the slippery slope.

- If you buy junk bonds, buy issues that are well known and that have good marketability. Small issues are hard to sell and you will be forced to take a concession in price.

- You increase your chances of default if you buy just one bond issue. Diversification is perhaps more important in this market than any other fixed-income investment.

- If you cannot devote the time to selecting high-yielding bonds, purchase shares in a mutual fund devoted to junk bonds.
- Do not, under any circumstances, put more than 10 percent of your total portfolio in high-yielding bonds!

S · H · O · R · T · C · U · T

High-Yield Bond Funds

- Cigna High Income Shares
- CIM High Yield Securities
- Kemper High Income Trust
- New America High Income
- Prospect Street High Income Portfolio
- Zenith Income

· 10 ·

Planning Your Portfolio

The fixed-income world is difficult to understand. After all, there are tens of thousands of issues, all with their own yields, their own characteristics and ratings, and their own redemption dates. Selecting the right debt instrument is undeniably time-consuming and not without effort.

Perhaps the first thing to keep in mind is that there is no one best investment, no highest-yielding instrument, no best return for all seasons. In the world of fixed-income investing, where the dominant characteristic is inconsistency and virtual unpredictability of interest rates, you are forever shooting at a moving target. Before taking aim, you need to have a strategy but no strategy is capable of handling all the variables at all times. What a strategy can do for you is to give a sense of coherence and a plan of action, especially for those times when uncertainty and indecision rule.

Your strategy depends totally on your personal situation. Two criteria should guide you on planning your portfolio of fixed-income investments.

1. The needs of you and your family should indicate how much periodic fixed income is necessary and desirable
2. The level of risk you are willing to tolerate to obtain that interest income

All fixed-income investments earn interest. You have loaned the borrower money, and in return the issuer of the debt obligation promises to pay back your principal and a rate of interest. However, interest may be paid monthly, quarterly, semiannually, annually or at the end of a given period. The following is a list of investment strategies to consider based on how frequently you wish to receive interest.

- If you require monthly income, consider either open-end or closed-end bond funds that make monthly interest payments. Mortgage pass-through certificates also pay interest (and principal) on a monthly basis.

- Quarterly interest payments can be made by withdrawing funds from your money market mutual fund or your money market account every three months. These accounts earn interest daily, therefore you will not be penalized for an early withdrawal since there is no set maturity date. (Dividends on stocks are paid quarterly, but fixed payments are certain with only a limited group of blue-chip companies. Remember that even the most conservative utility companies are not obliged to pay dividends—however, they are obliged to pay interest on their bonds.) Three-month Treasury bills naturally mature every 90 days.

- Semiannual interest payments are the rule for most bonds—be they corporate, Treasury, municipal or convertible. However, while most pay twice a year, in January and July, some bonds pay interest at other times of the year.

- Annual fixed-income investments, such as one-year certificates of deposit or time deposits, return your interest and principal at the end of the term. One-year Treasury bills pay interest (the discount) at the start of the period, but the principal at the end.

- Some instruments—zero coupon bonds and U.S. saving bonds—pay no periodic interest. Interest accumulates and is paid when the bonds mature.

If you need periodic interest payments to maintain your standard of living, be sure to purchase instruments with the appropriate payment schedules. If possible, try to invest in long-term debt, since they normally pay the highest rates of interest. You can buy long-term debt for the best rates, but stagger your maturities. This is especially useful for families saving for college tuition— have some portion of the college fund mature each year when fees are to be paid. This strategy is also useful for retirees. Moreover, if your bonds mature sequentially, year after year, you avoid the problem of having to invest your whole portfolio when rates may be low.

Once you allow for the timely payment of interest, you must then consider your risk tolerance and how the various fixed-income investments fulfill your objectives. Table 10.1 illustrates some strong points of the various securities previously discussed. This information is, however, general; you must take the bond ratings into consideration. A triple A corporate bond must be thought of as relatively safe, while a B-rated bond is not. And, of course, bonds may well appreciate, depending at what price you buy them. However, if you buy them at or close to par there is less likelihood of appreciation unless interest rates fall. Conditions in the marketplace will always determine the specific characteristics of appreciation, income, and safety of any bond. Table 10.2, fixed-income investments are arranged in terms of risk. They are, of course, only suggestions; you must personalize your portfolio by adapting it to your circumstances. If your funds are limited, you may not be able to fill all the slots. These suggestions are meant to lead to immediate concrete steps. But they can also be

TABLE 10.1   Strengths of Selected Fixed-Income Investment
Instruments

Fixed-Income Investments	Goals		
	Appreciation	*Income*	*Safety*
U.S. savings bonds	X		X
U.S. Treasury bills, notes, bonds		X	X
U.S. agency securities		X	X
Mortgage pass-through securities	X	X	
Municipal bonds		X	X
Zero coupon bonds	X		X
Corporate bonds	X	X	
Convertible bonds	X	X	
Certificates of deposit		X	X
Money market account		X	X
Money market mutual fund		X	
Bond funds	X	X	
High-yielding bonds ("junk")	X	?	

viewed as goals to be reached when your savings for fixed-income investing increase.

It is best to obtain fixed-income investments when interest rates are high and prices low. As a rule, whenever the Treasury yield curve (found in your daily newspaper's business section) approaches or broaches double digits, it is probably a good time to allocate more funds to bonds. High interest rates generally make it impossible for the stock market to advance and almost always cause a business slow down (if not a full-blown recession).

The consequence of a business slowdown is usually lower rates and higher bond prices. Conversely, when yields are low, an investor should stay in short-term instruments (such as money market mutual funds and Treasury bills) while awaiting better opportunities. At that point in the business cycle, common stocks are more promising and funds should be allocated accordingly. In brief, bonds are

TABLE 10.2   Bond Investment Guide*

Risk-Tolerant		Age	
Children	*25–45 years*	*45–65 years*	*65-plus*
25% Zeros	25% Agency	15% High-yield	15% High-yield
25% US EE bonds	25% CV	15% Agency	25% MPT certificates
25% DD bonds	25% Corporate	20% CV	25% Treasury notes
25% High-yield	10% High-yield	25% Corporate	35% Corporate
	15% Zeros	25% Zeros	

Risk-Neutral		Age	
Children	*25–45 years*	*45–65 years*	*65-plus*
25% Zeros	25% Agency	25% Agency	25% Corporate
25% US EE bonds	25% Corporate	25% Corporate	25% MPT certificates
25% Muni bonds	25% CV	25% Zeros	25% Zeros
25% DD bonds	10% High-yield	25% CV	25% Treasury notes
	15% MMMF		

Risk-Averse		Age	
Children	*25–45 years*	*45–65 years*	*65-plus*
33% Zeros	25% Treasury notes	35% Treasury bonds	25% MPT certificates
33% US EE bonds	25% Muni bonds	15% Treasury bills	25% CD
33% Muni bond fund	25% Agency	25% Muni bonds	25% Muni bonds
	25% MMMF	25% Zeros	25% MMA

CD = Certificate of deposit
CV = Convertible bond
DD = Deep discount bond
MMA = Money market account
MMMF = Money market mutual fund
MPT = Mortgage pass-through certificates

---

*An account for children must consider the tax consequences of one of the provisions of the Tax Reform Act of 1986. The so-called kiddie tax mandated that earnings on funds in childrens' names be taxed at the parents' rate until the children reach the age of 14. To avoid the tax bite, funds saved for childrens' college tuition should emphasize growth of principal and de-emphasize fixed-income investments.

better investments at the end of the business cycle than they are the beginning of one.

Specifically, the following guidelines should help you select bonds with more precision:

DO'S

1. Before purchasing a bond, find out how well the issuer, whether it is a corporation or a municipality, has fared over the years and how it is expected to perform in the future. Always take the rating into consideration.
2. Make sure the investment vehicle you choose is the right one for you in terms of the risk, the payment schedule and the length of time to maturity.
3. Before you invest, make sure you fully understand all of the terms before parting with any money. If there is anything you do not understand, ask your broker, your banker or the issuer for an explanation. If you still don't understand it, forget it.
4. Compute the yield to maturity in order to determine exactly what your return will be.
5. If you decide to buy more speculative issues for their higher return, make sure your holdings are well diversified to spread the risk. Even when buying high-quality issues, diversify your holdings as much as you can. Higher yields mean higher risk.
6. Tax-exempt bonds are not for everyone. Make sure that your tax bracket is high enough to make the lower-yield tax-free bonds worthwhile.
7. Follow what is happening in the financial markets by reserving some time each day, if only a few minutes, to read the financial section of a good newspaper.

DON'TS

1. Do not buy on tips or hunches. Do your research.
2. Do not rush to your decision. Take the time to determine your objectives and to decide how best to satisfy them. It is worth sacrificing a small amount of income for a time in order to avoid big mistakes.
3. Do not make any investments that you are not comfortable with. There are enough alternatives available that anyone should be able to find some investments that suit their financial (and emotional) needs.
4. Do not assume that there are no risks involved in fixed-income investments. Be informed of the risks so that you can act intelligently.
5. Do not buy low-quality issues unless you are in a position to afford the risks involved.

APPENDIX A
Yield to Maturity

The yield to maturity is the one calculated over time. It is not enough to know the coupon yield and the current yield, but what is the return of your funds to the time that the bond matures.

To calculate yield to maturity, you must realize that, generally speaking all issues come back to par (their face value, which is usually $1,000) when they are redeemed. If you have paid a premium (a purchase price over par) for a high-yielding bond, you will lose that premium by maturity. If you bought the bond at a discount, you can consider the difference between the discount price and the face value as additional yield.

Calculating a precise yield to maturity is not necessary, since every brokerage house and bank has tables of values. There are a couple of simple formulas which the investor can use without taxing one's arithmetic. These will give reasonably close approximations.

First, find the price change to maturity, whether plus (if bought at a discount) or minus (if bought at a premium). Then divide it by the number of years left to maturity to arrive at an adjustment percentage. If the purchase price is less than par, the adjustment is added to the current yield. If the bought price is more than par, the adjustment is subtracted.

For example, a bond bought at discount with the following features:

Coupon:	6%
Maturity:	5 years
Price:	84
Current yield:	7.14%

The difference between the par value (100) and the purchase price (84) is 16. Divide 16 by 5 years and the adjustment is 3.2 percent. With a price less than par, this adjustment is added to the current yield of 7.14 percent for a total of 10.34 percent. (The actual yield to maturity is 10.2 percent.)

If the bond had been bought at a premium:

Coupon:	10%
Maturity:	5 years
Price:	107
Current yield:	9.3%

In this case, the difference between par and the purchase price is 7. Divide 7 by 5 years and the adjustment is 1.4 percent. With a price more than par, this adjustment is subtracted from the current yield of 9.3 percent for a near yield to maturity of 7.9 percent. (The actual yield to maturity is 8.3 percent.)

What is clear from the yield to maturity is that even though the premium bond had a higher current yield (9.3 percent as against 7.1 percent), the discount bond had a higher yield to maturity. If you wanted high current income, you would have bought the premium bond. Conversely, the discounted bond would lower current income (and presumably taxes), but produce larger future gains.

Another way of calculating the yield to maturity is a bit more precise. For the same discounted bond, assuming the same values:

$$\frac{\text{Coupon rate} + \text{Average year discount}}{(\text{Par value} + \text{Purchase price}) \div 2}$$

$$\frac{60 + 32}{(\$1,000 + \$800) \div 2} = 10.2\%$$

In the case of the premium bond, assuming the same values:

$$\frac{100 - 14}{(\$1,000 + \$1,070) \div 2} = 8.31\%$$

Financial calculators are available with pre-programmed bond tables to calculate yield to maturity.

Since yield to maturity is a common denominator, all bonds tend to be quoted on that basis. Remember that yield to maturity represents the total present value of all coupon payments until redemption, plus the present value of the face amount of the bond at the maturity date. Or to put it slightly differently, the yield to maturity is the discount rate in a present value calculation which makes all cash payments over the bond's remaining life (coupon payments and principal) equal to the bond's market value.

Make sure that the yield to maturity is quoted to you when you are considering purchasing bonds. Only with that figure can you know precisely what amount of interest the bonds will earn.

APPENDIX B
*Characteristics of Selected
Fixed-Income Investments*

Issue	Gov't Guarantee		Taxable Federal	
	Yes	*No*	*Yes*	*No*
Money Market				
Accounts-banks	X		X	
Funds		X	X	
Certificates of Deposit	X		X	
Convertible Bonds		X	X	
U.S. Treasury				
Bills	X		X	
Notes	X		X	
Bonds	X		X	
U.S. Savings				
Bonds				
EE series	X		X	
HH series	X		X	
U.S. Agencies Notes and Bonds				
Federal Home Loan Bank		X	X	
Banks for Cooperatives		X	X	
Federal Land Banks		X	X	
Federal Intermediate Credit Bank		X	X	
Mortgage-Backed Pass-Throughs				
Government National Mortgage As.	X		X	
Federal National Mortgage As.		X	X	
Federal Home Loan Mortgage Corporation		X	X	
Corporate Bonds		X	X	
Municipal Bonds				
Pre Aug. 15 '86 general oblig.	X			X
Revenue		X		X
After Aug. 15 '86				
Public purpose	X			X
Priv't purpose	X		X	X
Nongovernment	X			X
			Preference‡	
Zero Coupon Bonds				
U.S. STRIPS	X		X	
Municipals	X			X
Private	X		X	

*EE Series savings bond: Face value $50, $100 and up to $10,000.

†HH series savings bond: Obtainable only by converting EE series savings bonds, minimum $500.

‡Preference item: Taxable only when calculating the alternative minimum tax.

§Deep discount: The price is far below face value of the bond.

Taxable City/State		Minimum Investment				
Yes	*No*	*$500*	*$1,000*	*$5,000*	*$10,000*	*$25,000*
X			Any Amount			
X			X			
X		X	X			
X			X			
	X				X	
	X			X		
	X		X			
	X	−X*				
	X	X†				
	X				X	
	X			X		
	X		X			
	X			X		
X						X
X						X
X						X
X			X			
	X			X		
	X			X		
				X		
				X		
				X		
	X		Deep Disc.§			
	X		Deep Disc.§			
X			Deep Disc.§			

Glossary

accrued interest   The interest that has accumulated since the last payment date of a bond.

asked price   Also called the *offer*, this is the lowest price at which a holder is willing to sell a security at a given time.

basis point   A minimum measurement in a financial transaction—1/100 of 1 percent.

bearer bond   A bond that does not have the owner's name registered on its face or on the issuer's books. The person having a bearer bond in his or her possession is considered to be the owner. Interest and principal are payable to the holder, and no endorsement is required on transfers. Although tax law changes enacted in 1982 effectively prohibit the issuance of new bonds in bearer form, already outstanding bearer bonds may be purchased on the secondary market.

bid price   The highest price a buyer is willing to pay for a security at a given time.

bond   A secured promissory note that represents the issuer's pledge to pay back the principal at face value on a specific date. Until that date, the issuer generally agrees to pay a fixed amount of interest at semiannual intervals. The term *bond* is frequently applied to other types of fixed-income instruments that technically are not bonds at all.

bondholder   A creditor of the issuing municipality or company through the ownership of a bond. Unlike a stockholder, he or she does not have an equity interest in the corporation.

book entry   *See* registered bond.

business cycle   The alternating phases of business conditions that range from boom to bust. A typical business cycle has five phases: revival, expansion, maturation, contraction and recession.

callable bond   A bond issue that may be redeemed, in whole or in part, for cash, at the discretion of the issuer within certain limits of price and time.

call provision   *See* callable bond.

capital gains (losses)   The profit (or loss) from the sale of an investment or capital asset above (or below) the purchase price.

certificate of deposit   A type of interest-bearing debt instrument that is issued by banking institutions.

collateralized trust bond   A bond that has collateral pledged to guarantee repayment of principal.

commercial paper   A type of unsecured short-term negotiable debt instrument sold at a discount by corporate issuers.

company risk   Business conditions are always uncertain, and all corporations are subject to the vicissitudes of their markets. Investors in the corporate bond market may find their investments impacted by business conditions even though they are creditors, not owners.

conversion price   The price that a convertible bond (or preferred stock) can be exchanged for common stock of the corporation.

convertible bond   A special type of corporate bond that can be exchanged by the holder at his or her discretion for a specified number of common shares of the issuing corporation.

coupon rate   The amount of interest a bond issuer has pledged to pay the bondholder annually.

current yield   The percentage return on a bond calculated by dividing the annual interest payments by the present price of the bond. For example, a 13 percent $1,000 par value bond selling at $950 offers a current yield of 13.7 percent ($130 ÷ $950 = 13.7 percent).

debenture   An unsecured, long-term debt obligation issued by a corporation. The debenture is issued against the general credit of the corporation, rather than against a specific asset.

deep discount bond (original issue) An issue of bonds sold at a deep discount from its par value. The coupon rate is low compared to prevailing interest rates.

default Failure to perform a contractual obligation, particularly the payment of interest or principal on debt at a stated date.

deflation A decline in general prices that has the effect of increasing purchasing power.

discount The amount by which a bond is selling below its par value.

discount rate The rate the Federal Reserve System charges to member banks for loans. It is a rate that the Fed changes to tighten and ease the money supply.

disinflation A decline in the rate of inflation.

effective yield This is the actual yield on an investment after allowing for compounding over a period of time, in contrast to the nominal or stated rate.

equipment trust certificate A debt obligation utilized by corporations in the transportation business. These certificates are secured by specific equipment, such as railroad cars.

federal funds rate The interest rate charged by banks on their excess reserve funds to banks that are deficient in their reserve positions.

first mortgage bond A bond secured by a first lien on specified properties of the issuer, such as buildings and land.

fixed-income investment Any debt obligation that returns to the investor or depositor a set sum (interest) on a regular basis whether it be monthly, quarterly, semiannually or annually. This broad category encompasses time deposits in banks, money market instruments (such as commercial paper issued by corporations, money market accounts and funds) and bonds. The term also applies to bonds (such as zero coupon bonds) and certificates of deposit that pay interest at maturity or at the end of their term.

general obligation bond A bond issued by a state or political subdivision that is backed by the full faith and credit (taxing power) of the issuer.

Ginnie Mae certificate A debt instrument of the Government National Mortgage Association (GNMA) that is backed by a "full faith and credit" guarantee of the U.S. government. Issued in minimum denominations of $25,000 with $5,000 increments, such certificates represent an interest in a pool of mortgages insured by the Federal Housing Authority (FHA) or the Veterans Administration (VA). Owners of the certificates receive monthly checks, each consisting partly of interest and partly of principal. Although Ginnie Mae certificates typically have life spans of 30 years, FHA statistical studies have shown that the average life of mortgages in the pools is about 12 years because of prepayments.

high-yielding bond   A debt obligation that provides a rate of interest far exceeding average rates of return. These are almost always speculative bonds and have high rates of default. They are commonly referred to as "junk" bonds, but there are hundreds of these issues—some are better than others.

income bond   A bond on which interest is paid only from the profit of the issuing corporation. Such bonds usually are issued in reorganization proceedings.

indenture   A written agreement between the corporation and the creditors for the issuance of bonds stating interest rate, redemption date, priorities of claims and other relevant matters.

industrial development bond   A tax-exempt bond whose interest and principal payments are backed by a private corporation.

interest   The price paid for borrowed funds, the "rent" for money.

interest rate risk   Fluctuations of capital caused by the rise and fall of interest rates. The inverse relationship of principal to interest rates means that when interest rates rise, principal falls and vice versa. All negotiable fixed-income investments are subject to interest-rate risk.

inverted yield curve   An atypical yield curve indicating that short-term interest rates are higher than long-term ones. An inverted yield curve often presages a business slowdown or a recession.

investment-grade bond   Any bond ranked as AAA, AA, A, or BBB.

junk bond   *See* high-yielding bond.

leverage   The use of large amounts of borrowed funds. This enhances the earnings per share of common stock after interest payments are made. However, leverage can work the other way as well, leaving nothing to the common stockholder if earnings do not cover interest charges.

leveraged buyout The acquisition of a corporation, usually assisted by the use of high-yield bonds.

liquidity The ability of a business to change its assets into cash without any loss. Measurements of liquidity attest to a corporation's health. In the securities market, liquidity is the ability to transact purchases and sales without any significant concession in price.

market risk All businesses (and governmental bonds to some degree) are effected by system-wide events in the economy. It is difficult to define exactly what constitutes market risk, but some past examples are a stock market crash, a presidential assassination, or an act of war—events that had national or global ramifications.

maturity The date at which a debt obligation must be repaid by the issuer.

money market account A demand deposit bank account that pays interest comparable to money mark instruments such as commercial paper, bankers' acceptances and Treasury bills.

money market fund A type of mutual fund that specializes in investments in short-term debt instruments, including government paper, commercial paper issued by corporations and bank certificates of deposit.

mortgage-backed security *See* Ginnie Mae certificate.

mutual fund Also known as an open-end investment company, the mutual fund invests pooled cash of numerous investors in a managed portfolio designed to meet the fund's stated objectives. Mutual funds generally stand ready to sell and redeem their shares at any time at the current net asset value per share.

negotiable instrument Any security that can be freely exchanged for money such as a stock, bond, check or draft.

net asset value All of the assets of a mutual fund minus all of the liabilities. The net asset value is frequently expressed on a per-share basis.

no-load fund A mutual fund that does not impose a sales charge or commission on its shares. Some funds are back-loaded, that is, they charge no sales charge on purchase, but charge a fee should the purchaser sell the shares before a given period of years.

note   A debt obligation, usually unsecured and frequently with a maturity of five years or less at the time of issue.

par value   The face value of a bond, usually but not always $1,000.

preference item   A nontaxable source of income, which must be included in calculating the alternative minimum tax.

premium   The amount by which a bond sells in excess of its par value.

prospectus   A document prepared by the issuer or the underwriter of a security, which gives a detailed description of the operations and financial history of the issuer, plus the terms and conditions of the security being offered. The document must be filed with the Securities and Exchange Commission, and must be provided to potential purchasers of a new securities issue in order to enable them to evaluate the issue and make a decision on its purchase.

put bond   A bond issued with a special feature allowing the investor to redeem the security at a stated rate for a certain time.

rate of return   The yield obtained on an investment based on its purchase price.

refunding bond   A bond issued to retire another bond outstanding.

registered bond   A bond that has the name of its owners or the owner's agent written on its face and recorded on the books of the issuer. Ownership may be transferred only by the owner or agent.

return on investment   *See* rate of return.

risk   A condition in the investment world that precludes a predictable or certain outcome. In fixed-income investments, some instruments are risk-free, such as U.S. government obligations and time deposits in banks, while the rest contain some element of chance. The amount of risk is measured by the rating agencies. In the stock market virtually all investments have some risk, that is the outcome of the investment is uncertain. Risk, of course, means the possibility of loss of funds.

risk-averse   Risk-averse investors wish to avoid chancy situations and possibility of loss. They insist on knowing the interest rate, the yield and the maturity or redemption date.

risk lover   Some investors welcome chance, since it implies greater than average rewards.

risk-neutral Risk-neutral investors neither welcome risk or shun it. They are willing to tolerate some level of chance in their return on their investment portfolios.

seasoned issues Bonds that have already been issued and exposed to the various influences of the credit market.

secondary market For fixed-income investments, the bond markets of the New York Stock Exchange, the American Stock Exchange or the over-the-counter market that facilitate trades after the original issue has been underwritten by investment bankers.

senior securities Bonds and preferred issues that receive consideration before common stock in case of a bankruptcy or other financial difficulties.

serial bond A bond issue made up of various series with staggered maturity dates, frequently at intervals of six months or one year.

sinking fund A fund created by setting aside a specified amount of money at regular intervals in order to provide for repayment of part or all of a debt issue.

spread The difference between two prices. The term is frequently used in reference to the difference between the bid and asked price for a security.

term bond A bond issue that comes due all at once rather than serially.

tombstone An advertisement in the financial press, placed by underwriters, indicating the sale of securities. The underwriting investment banks, the syndicate, are all listed in order of importance.

Treasury bill A debt obligation of the U.S. government with a maturity of 52 weeks or less from the date of issue. T-bills are sold at a discount, and your return is the difference between the purchase price and the face value that is repaid at maturity.

Treasury bond A long-term debt obligation of the U.S. government having a maturity of seven years or more from the date of issue. Interest is at a fixed rate, payable semiannually.

Treasury note A U.S. government debt obligation with a maturity of not less than one nor more than seven years from the date of issue. Otherwise, it is identical to a Treasury bond.

trustee   A person or institution who owns or administers property for the benefit of an individual or class of individuals.

underwriter   Also known as an investment banker, the underwriter is an intermediary between corporations or municipalities issuing new securities and the individuals or institutions to which the issue is sold. The underwriter is responsible for ultimate sale of the issue and either buys the whole issue and resells it to investors or forms a group to sell the bonds.

unit investment trust   A vehicle sponsored by brokerage firms that invests the pooled funds of many investors in a fixed portfolio of interest-bearing securities. Units usually can be purchased for $1,000.

yield   The rate of return received from an investment, usually expressed annually.

yield curve   The graphic representation of interest rates (usually for Treasury securities) over a period of time—from tomorrow to 30 years.

yield to maturity   The yield on a bond, taking into consideration the price paid, the interest to be received and the principal amount to be repaid at maturity.

zero coupon bond   A deep discount bond that bears no coupons. The return is based on the difference between the purchase price and the principal amount repaid at maturity.

Index

Active investor, xvi, 37
Agency securities. *See* Federal
    agency securities
Agricultural debt, 72–73
Alternative minimum tax, 88–89,
    91
American Capital Convertible, 130
American Municipal Bond
    Assurance Corporation, 92
Appreciation, 142
"Arithmetic of Interest Rates,"
    18–19
Asset allocation, xviii
AT&T, 14
Auctions, Treasury, 56–57
Axe-Houghton Income Fund, 121

Bancroft Convertible, 130
Bank for Cooperatives, 72–73
Bank Rate Monitor, 39
Basis Book, 96
Basis points, 63, 70
Bearer bonds, 94–95
Bellwether indicators, 58
Benham Treasury Note Fund, 66
Blue List, The, 95
Bond Buyer, 95
Bond Guide, 95
Bond indenture, 20, 105
Bond investment guide, 143
Bond Investors Association, 136

Bonds
    See also specific types of
        bonds
    behavior of, 7–14
    defined, 1–3
    reasons for investing in, 4–7
Bond Survey, 109
Business cycle, and bond prices,
    12–14

Call protection, 85
Call provisions, 3
Capital gains, 6
Castle Convertible, 130
CATS, 61
CD basis, 26
Certificates of Accrual on Treasury
    Securities (CATS), 61
Certificates of deposit, 42–45, 140
Children, taxation of, 142
Cigna High Income Shares, 138
Cigna Income Fund, 121
CIM High Yield Securities, 138
Collateralized trust bonds, 104
College savings, 46, 63, 141, 142
Company risk, xv
Compound interest, xii, 26, 35
    and simple interest
        compared, 18–19
Compound interest bonds, 98
Computerized data bases, xv
Consolidated Federal Farm Loan
    bonds, 73

Conversion parity, 128
Conversion ratio, 127
Conversion value, 127–28
Convertible bonds, 123–30, 140
  case for, 126–28
  funds, 130
Convertible zeros, 97
Corporate bonds, 103–21, 140
  See also Junk bonds
  buying and selling, 109–12
  description, 103–7
  discount, 119
  evaluations, 115–17
  event risk, 117–19
  funds, 121
  pricing, 112–13
  ratings, 113–15
  reasons for issuing, 107–9
Coupon rate, 2, 27
Coupon yield, 2, 20, 85
Credit ratings
  for convertible bonds, 124
  for corporate bonds, 113–17
  for junk bonds, 132
  for municipal bonds, 92–94
Creditwatch, 109
CreditWeek, 95
Creditworthiness, and bond prices, 10–12
Current yield, 2, 3, 20–21

Debentures, 70, 104
Deflation, 12
Deregulation of financial markets, 4–5
Discount, 3, 119
Discount rate, 9, 30
Disinflation, 12
Diversification, importance of, 7, 137
Dollar bonds, 95
Double-barreled bonds, 91
Dreyfus Tax-Exempt Bond Fund, 101
Drexel Burnham Lambert, 134

Early call provision, 85
EE series savings bonds, 46
Effective yield, 44
Ellsworth Convertible Growth and Income, 130
Equipment trust certificates, 105
Equivalent bond yield, 27
Event risk, 117–19
Expansion stage, 13

Fannie Mae, 70, 72, 74, 76, 77
  pricing securities, 75
Farm credit agencies, 72–73
Federal agency securities, 69–81
  agricultural debt, 72–73
  description, 70–71
  funds, 81
  home mortgage securities, 74–75
  mortgage-backed securities, 76–79, 80
  pricing, 75–76
Federal Deposit Insurance Corporation, 39
Federal Farm Credit system, 73
Federal funds rate, 13
Federal Home Loan Banks, 70, 71, 74
Federal Home Loan Mortgage Association (FHLMC), 76
Federal Intermediate Credit Banks, 72–73
Federal Land Banks, 70, 72–73
Federal National Mortgage Association (FNMA), 70, 72, 74, 76, 77
  pricing securities, 75
Federal Reserve Board, 9–10
Federated Tax-Free Income Yield, 101
Fidelity Government Securities Fund, 66
Fixed-income investor profile, xvii
FPA New Income, 81
Freddie Mac, 76, 77
"Full faith and credit" pledge, 49

General obligation bonds, 83, 84,
91
General obligation public purpose
bonds, 90
Ginnie Mae, 70, 72, 74, 76, 77, 79
Government bond funds, 66–67
Government bonds. *See* U.S.
Treasury securities
Government National Mortgage
Association (GNMA), 70, 72,
74, 76, 77, 79

HH series savings bonds, 46
High-yield corporate bonds. *See*
Junk bonds
Housing bonds, 92

Income, investing for, xvii, 142.
See also Income bonds
Income bonds, 116, 120, 140
Indenture, 1
Inflation, 12, 29
Insured bonds, 92
Inter-American Development
Bank, 70
Interest
investment strategies for,
140–41
on municipal bonds, 96–98
Interest rate risk, xv
convertible bonds, 124
corporate bonds, 106
federal agency securities, 78
Interest rates, xii–xiv, 9–10
See also Interest; Interest
rate risk
and yield curve, 28–34
Inverted yield curve, 32–33
Investment grade ratings,
municipal bonds, 92–93
Investment guide, 143
Investment value, 126

John Hancock Tax-Exempt
Income, 101

Junk bonds, 4, 35, 118, 131–38
funds, 138
Kemper High Income Trust, 138
Kemper Income & Capital
Preservation, 121

Leveraged buyouts, 129, 132
Lexington GNMA Income, 81
Lieberman, Charles, 33
Limited bonds, 91
Lincoln National Convertible, 130
Liquidity, 14
Long-term bond market, 31
Lord Abbett U.S. Government
Securities, 66

Mandatory put, 92
Market risk, xv
Maturation stage, 13
M-CATS, 62
Merrill Lynch, 61
Merrill Lynch Federal Securities,
81
Money Fund Report, 39
Money market accounts, 38–40,
47, 140
Money market funds, 40–42, 47,
140
Money supply, 13
Monroe Trader, 96
Mortgage-backed securities, 18,
76–79, 80
Municipal Bond Book, 95
Municipal Bond Investors
Assurance Corporation, 92
Municipal bonds, 10, 83–101, 140
buying, 94–96
categories of, 90–92
described, 83–87
funds, 101
interest on, 96–98, 149
investment grade ratings,
92–93
speculative grade ratings,
93–94

swapping, 98–99
tax exemption benefits,
87–90
Municipal multipliers, 98
Municipal Receipts, 62
Mutual funds, 40–42

Negotiable instruments, 8
Net worth statement, x
New America High Income, 138
New Jersey Hackensack Water, 14
Nominal rate, 44
Nominal yield, 2
Nongovernmental-purpose bonds,
90–91, 100
Normal yield curve, 31
Notes, U.S. Treasury, 55–60

Optional put, 92
Original issue deep discount
bonds, 25, 119
Paid-down certificates, 79
Par value, 1, 23
Passive investor, xvi
Pass-through certificates, 76
Portfolio planning, 139–45
selecting bonds, 144–45
Preference items, 86, 89, 91
Premium, 2–3
Prevailing interest rates, 21–22
Price, T. Rowe Tax-Free Income
Fund, 101
Princor Government Securities
Income, 81
Private activity bonds, 90, 100
Prospect Street High Income
Portfolio, 138
Put bonds, 85, 92
Putnam U.S. Government
Guaranteed Securities, 67

Recession, 13, 33
Refunded bonds, 92
Reinvestment rate, 24–25
Retirement savings, 62, 63, 141
Return on investment, 17

Revenue bonds, 83, 84, 91
Revival stage, 13
Risk, xiii–xvi
and convertible bonds, 124
and corporate bonds, 105–6
in federal agency securities,
78
and junk bonds, 132
and municipal bonds, 84
Risk-free investments, 37–47,
49–55, 71
certificates of deposit, 42–45
federal agency securities, 71
money market accounts,
38–40
money market funds, 40–42
RJR Nabisco leveraged buyout,
118–19

Safety, investing for, xvii, 142
Salomon Brothers, 61
Savings bonds, U.S., 45–46
Savings plan, x–xii
Scudder Income Fund, 121
Senior securities, 1
Separate Trading of Registered
Interest and Principal of
Securities (STRIPS), 61
Serial bonds, 84, 95
Simple vs. compound interest,
18–19
Sinking fund, 3
SLH Income-Mortgage Securities,
81
Smith Barney Monthly
Government, 81
Special tax bonds, 91
Speculative grade ratings,
municipal bonds, 93–94
Statistical rating agencies, xv
SteinRoe High-Yield Municipals,
101
Stocks. *See* Convertible bonds
STRIPS, 61
Student Loan Marketing, 70
Subordinate debentures, 104

Swapping, municipal bonds, 98–99
T. Rowe Price Tax-Free Income
    Fund, 101
Tax changes, and bond market, 6
Tax-deferred interest securities, 97
Tax-free investing, 83–101
Tax Reform Act of 1986, 6
    kiddie tax, 142
    and municipal bonds, 86–88,
        90
T-bills, 27–28, 49–55
TCW Convertible Securities, 130
Term bonds, 84, 95
TIGRS, 61
Time deposits, 140
Tombstone, 108, 110
Total rate of return, 19, 24–25
Trainer, Richard D.C., 18
Treasury Investment Growth
    Receipts (TIGRS), 61
Treasury securities. *See* U. S.
    Treasury securities
Trustee, 1
Trust indenture, 108

U.S. savings bonds, 45–46, 141
U.S. Treasury securities
    auctions of, 9–10
    bills, 27–28, 49–55
    notes and bonds, 55–60, 140
    savings bonds, 45–46
    zero coupon bonds, 60–65

Value Line U.S. Government
    Securities, 67
Vanguard Fixed
    Income—Investment Grade, 121
Van Kampen Merritt U.S.
    Government, 67
Volatility, of zero coupon bonds, 64

Wasatch Income, 121
Wash sale, 99
World Bank, 70

Yield, bond, 2, 14, 17–35
    inequality of various, 26–28
    kinds of, 19–24
    total return, 24–25
Yield Book, 96
Yield curve, and interest rates,
    28–34
Yield to maturity, 2, 3, 22–24, 85,
    96
    calculating, 147–49

Zenith Income, 138
Zero corporate bonds, 62
Zero coupon bonds, 25, 60–65, 66,
    141
Zero municipal bonds, 62, 97